CO-AWJ-453

DATE DUE

POLICY STUDIES IN EMPLOYMENT AND WELFARE NUMBER 37

General Editor: Sar A. Levitan

The Wage Bargain
and the Labor Market

H. M. Douty

The Johns Hopkins University Press
Baltimore and London

The Johns Hopkins University Press, Baltimore, Maryland 21218
The Johns Hopkins Press Ltd., London

Library of Congress Cataloging in Publication Data

Douty, Harry Mortimer, 1909–
  The wage bargain and the labor market.

  (Policy studies in employment and welfare; no. 37)

  Includes bibliographical references and index.
  1. Wages—United States.   2. Non-wage payments—
United States.   3. Labor supply—United States.
I. Title.
HD4975.D628   331.2'973   79–3720
ISBN 0–8018–2393–5
ISBN 0–8018–2394–3 (pbk.)

FOR ESTHER

Contents

Tables

The Wage Bargain and the Labor Market

1

Introduction

The expression "wage bargain" embraces the rates of pay and other elements of compensation, such as employer contributions to pension and insurance plans, that workers obtain in exchange for labor services. The terms of the bargain may reflect the outcome of negotiations between worker and employer representatives, or, in nonunion firms, the acceptance of terms established by employer personnel policy. The latter situation does not imply helplessness on the part of the worker, provided there is competition in the labor market and the worker has access to a number of different employers. In recent decades, the federal government, through statutory minimum wage determinations, has played a direct role in the wage-setting process, and in other ways has entered into the functioning of the labor market.

As a component of national income, employee compensation in 1978 amounted to about $1.3 trillion, of which $1.1 trillion was paid out as direct wages and salaries, the remainder representing employer contributions for legally required social insurance and for private pension and insurance programs. Labor compensation thus represented somewhat more than three-fourths (76.4 percent) of national income. The balance was accounted for by the income of farm and nonfarm proprietors, and by the rental income of persons, net interest, and corporate profits.

Wages and salaries are, in effect, prices, and hence, in the absence of the direction of labor by some central authority, are subject to forces affecting labor demand and supply. If this were not so, the notion of a labor market would have little meaning. Among the important functions performed by wages in a market economy is the exertion of substantial influence on the allocation of labor among occupations and industries so as to maximize, at least in an approximate way, the volume and variety of goods and services that consumers want to purchase.

The thousands of wage bargains that are concluded each year largely determine the living standards that most Americans can maintain. Changes in the level of money wages, when adjusted for changes in consumer prices, provide insight into the alteration that occurs in that standard over periods of time. Moreover, the wage determination process, in establishing relative prices for the varying skills and abilities required in production, helps to form decisions with respect to education and training for existing and oncoming members of the labor force.

There are particular social and institutional forces that impinge upon the operation of the labor market, as compared with other kinds of markets, and that serve to complicate explanation of wage determination. For a number of reasons, adjustments in the labor market to changes in the supply or demand for workers with particular experience, training, or skill are often difficult and time-consuming.

Wages, while representing income for workers, constitute cost for employers. This is the essential link between wages and employment. An employer will expect to recover the wages of his employees in the prices of the goods or services they produce, normally in conjunction at any given time, with fixed quantities of capital. Hence, the demand for labor, for the most part, is derived from the demand for the final product or products of the enterprise, and not for itself alone. The theory of the demand for labor, on the basis of various assumptions relating to the character of product markets, has been worked out with great elegance by economists over roughly the past hundred years.

Wages are not of course determined by demand alone, for labor supply schedules must be reckoned with and institutional factors, such as trade unionism, taken into account. But employment decisions are related to the wage levels for workers of particular grades and skills

2

that confront employers and to which they must adjust over shorter or longer periods. Changes in relative wages among occupations, firms, or industries, or general wage changes in the economy as a whole, can affect the structure and level of employment. This consequence is often difficult to detect in a dynamic and growing economy, but it does exist.

This monograph is not intended in any sense to present a systematic exposition of wage theory, for which readings are suggested at the end of this chapter. It is intended, rather, to provide a broad review of the nature and outcome of the wage determination process in the United States, as the following outline of its contents indicates.

The major elements in the wage bargain, with particular reference to the rise of employer-financed benefits that supplement basic rates of pay, are discussed briefly in Chapter 2. Chapter 3 deals with the labor market as providing the principal mechanism through which wages are determined, with emphasis upon some of the ways in which the forces operating within labor markets differ from those that affect prices in other types of markets.

Attention is directed in Chapter 4 to the immense variety of skills or occupations in the United States to which wage or salary rates must be attached, and an effort is made to indicate the general dimensions of the occupational wage structure that presently has emerged. But a wage structure, in the sense of a series or hierarchy of rates of pay, is not immutable. It responds, often haltingly, to underlying changes in supply and demand in the labor market. Chapter 5 seeks to throw light on the broad changes that have occurred in the structure of relative wages in the United States during the present century. The discussion of relative wages (that is, of wage structure) is largely, and necessarily, in terms of average rates of pay. But in practically all occupations, even within local labor markets, there is substantial dispersion of rates of pay around the average levels. The intriguing question of wage dispersion within occupations is considered in Chapter 6.

It is through the wage mechanism that the general standard of living is basically determined for the nonfarm working population. Chapter 7 attempts briefly to trace the movement of money and real wages over the period since 1800, including a discussion of the key role of productivity in accounting for changes in the level of real wages. This heroic effort is followed, in Chapter 8, by a discussion of the forces making for general wage change, with reference particularly to the period since World War II. Included is an analysis of the role of wage expectations that developed during this period and of the long and continuing inflation beginning in 1966.

Comparatively brief treatment is given in separate chapters to two important factors that have influenced post-World War II wage developments. The first of these, dealt with in Chapter 9, is trade unionism, which became established firmly during the postwar period as a major labor market institution in strategic sectors of the economy. Chapter 10 considers minimum wage actions under the Federal Fair Labor Standards Act. Finally, some concluding observations are ventured in Chapter 11.

The analysis that follows, except for the discussion in Chapter 2 of the elements of the wage bargain, runs largely in terms of rates of pay, or of some approximate measure of rates, rather than of rates plus employer expenditures on supplementary benefits. Rates of pay remain at the heart of the wage bargain. Moreover, most of the available data on the trend of wages, as well as statistical data on wages by occupation, relate to rates or earnings rather than to the total compensation package. Nevertheless, as the following chapter indicates, the growth of employer-financed benefits has been an important feature of wage development during the period following World War II. The increase in employer expenditures on benefits per hour of work appears to have been more rapid, taking the postwar period as a whole, than the increase in wage rates alone. This fact needs to be kept in mind in appraising wage developments during the postwar period.[1]

Suggested Readings

For a good review of the present state of wage theory, see Albert Rees's *The Economics of Work and Pay* (New York: Harper & Row, 1973), especially parts 1 and 2. Also most useful is Allan Cartter's *Theory of Wages and Employment* (Homewood, Ill.: Richard D. Irwin, 1959). J. R. Hicks's *The Theory of Wages,* 2d ed. (New York: St. Martin's Press, 1963), which first appeared in 1932, can still be read with profit, with due regard to the preface to the second edition.

2

Elements of the Wage Bargain

Basic Rates of Pay

Whether arrived at through collective or individual bargaining, wages are now likely to exhibit considerable complexity. This was not always so. Up to World Ware II, wages for most manual workers, and for many white-collar workers as well, could be described almost entirely in terms of rates of pay per hour, day, week, month, or year, or of earnings under piece-rate or other types of incentive wage systems. Rates for blue-collar workers usually were quoted by the hour or day; those for white-collar workers by the week, month, or, in the case of professional employees such as teachers, by the year.

Time rates, or earned rates under incentive pay systems,[1] may be defined as basic pay for a unit of time or output. They still constitute the heart of the labor bargain. But beginning in the latter half of the 1930s, a variety of supplements to basic wages began to assume significance in the American wage system. Such supplements provide additional money income, paid leisure, or income security to workers. They represent cost to employers.

Supplementary Benefits

Supplementary benefits may be grouped into three broad categories: premium pay, pay for time not worked, and employer contributions to insurance and pension plans.

Premium Pay

As a supplementary benefit, premium pay is most important for work performed beyond daily or weekly standard hours. The payment of premium rates for overtime was given enormous impetus by the passage of the federal Fair Labor Standards Act (1938). For covered workers, this act required the payment, beginning with the third year after its effective date, of time and one-half regular rates of pay for hours worked beyond 40 per week. Coverage of the act was broadened dramatically in 1961 and subsequently, so that currently more than three-fourths of all nonsupervisory workers in private employment are subject to its provisions. Premium pay practices more favorable than those required by law (e.g., for overtime hours on a daily basis or for nonscheduled work on weekends or holidays) are widely found in collective bargaining agreements.[2]

There are other types of premium pay. Extra pay for late-shift work is common. In petroleum refining, for example, approximately half of the industry's work force in 1976 was assigned to rotating shifts. Workers on evening schedules typically received 20 cents an hour above day rates, and those on night schedules 40 cents.[3] In nonferrous foundries, where about 18 percent of the workers were on second shift work in 1975, the size of the shift premium ranged widely, but with some concentrations at 10 cents an hour and at 5 percent above day rates.[4]

Workers called in at other than their normal reporting time frequently receive premium rates for the off-scheduled hours. In some industries, premium rates are paid for tasks that are especially heavy, disagreeable, or dangerous. Longshoremen, for instance, are paid premium rates for handling explosives and certain other types of cargo.

Premium pay, when earned, serves to increase the direct money income of workers. It can be viewed as a wage "supplement" in the sense that it is auxiliary to basic rates of pay; moreover, its widespread incorporation into the pay structure has occurred only since the late 1930s through legislation, collective bargaining, and employer personnel policy. In a sense, however, premium pay differs from the other types of supplements described below. It largely represents pay above straight-time rates for extra hours (or for inconvenient hours) worked at the behest of the employer, and this working time in some measure is under employer control and can be avoided.

Pay for Time Not Worked

A second major type of supplementary benefit consists of pay for time not worked. The widespread development of this category of benefits, especially for manual workers, owes much to the administration of wage controls by the National War Labor Board during World War II. As a safety-valve to the remarkably successful control of basic rates of pay, the board approved the adoption of several types of fringe benefits.[5] For example, paid vacations of one week after one year of service and two weeks after five years received virtually automatic approval in voluntary cases.[6] Paid sick leave plans, if reasonable in nature, were approved. Pay for holidays not worked was generally granted if in line with industry or area practice.

This type of "fringe benefit"—the term was invented in 1943—swiftly entered into the structure of labor compensation in American industry. Pay for time not worked was extended substantially during the postwar period. In particular, provisions for paid vacations and holidays spread rapidly, and their terms were liberalized. By 1975, virtually all plant and office workers in metropolitan areas, both union and nonunion, received vacation and holiday benefits, with provisions for office workers somewhat more liberal, on the average, than for plant workers.[7] Paid leave for personal and civic (e.g., jury duty) purposes was comparatively unimportant. Paid sick leave was confined largely to office workers.

Pension and Insurance Benefits

Employer expenditures for old-age pensions and for life, accident, and health insurance increased remarkably during the postwar period. These benefits in part are legally required, with federal social security and unemployment insurance programs dating from the 1930s. Workmen's compensation legislation had its origin earlier; by 1915 no fewer than 30 states had enacted laws for the compensation of workers for industrial injuries.

As in the case of vacation and holiday pay, the rise of private pension and especially of group insurance plans was given impetus by the World War II wage stabilization program. The spread of these plans was great stimulated, however, when the U.S. Supreme Court, in a 1949 case involving the United Steelworkers, held in effect that the Labor-Management Relations Act of 1947 required employers to bargain with unions on retirement and insurance plans. Following this decision, agreement on pension and insurance issues was reached between the Steelworkers and the major steel producers.

By 1975, insurance and pension plans, financed wholly or in part by employers, had become deeply embedded in the compensation structure for both plant and office workers in industry generally. For example, more than 90 percent of both groups of workers in metropolitan areas were covered by hospitalization, surgical, and medical programs; 78 percent of the plant workers and 86 percent of the office employees were in establishments with retirement plans.[8]

Composition of Employee Compensation

The most recent data developed by the Bureau of Labor Statistics on the relative importance of various elements of compensation of employees in the private nonfarm economy relate to 1974. These data are summarized in Table 2.1. It will be noticed that for both office and nonoffice workers, straight-time pay accounted for somewhat more than three-fourths of total compensation per hour worked. The *relative* importance of the various items of supplementary compensation varied among the two broad groups of employees. Paid leave and retirement programs, for example, were relatively more important items in the pay package for office than for nonoffice workers; insurance and health benefit programs, on the other hand, constituted a relatively greater proportion of compensation for nonoffice workers.

For office and nonoffice employees combined, premium pay added slightly less than 2 percent to total compensation; paid leave, mainly for vacations and holidays, 6.7 percent; and nonproduction bonuses, 1.5 percent. These items, when added to straight-time pay, constituted "gross payroll"—that is, direct money payments to employees before deductions for income tax, union dues, or other purposes. This represented 86.4 percent of total compensation in 1974. It should be noted that several items included in gross payroll, notably premium pay and pay for time not worked, were earlier designated as supplementary benefits on the ground that they represented additions to straight-time pay for working hours and historically are comparatively recent elements of compensation.

Table 2.1. Composition of Employee Compensation, Office and Nonoffice
Employees, Private Nonfarm Economy, 1974

| | Percentage of compensation per hour worked | | |
Item	All employees	Office employees	Nonoffice employees
Total Compensation	100.0	100.0	100.0
Pay for time worked	78.2	76.8	79.5
Straight-time pay	76.3	76.1	76.5
Premium pay	1.9	.7	3.0
Paid leave (including sick leave)	6.7	7.6	5.8
Retirement programs	8.1	8.4	7.8
Social security	4.4	4.0	4.8
Private plans	3.7	4.4	3.0
Life insurance and health benefit programs	4.2	3.3	5.1
Unemployment benefit programs	1.1	0.8	1.3
Nonproduction bonuses	1.5	2.8	0.4
Savings and thrift plans	0.2	0.4	0.1
Wages and salaries (gross payroll)*	86.4	87.2	85.7
Supplements to wages and salaries†	13.6	12.8	14.3

Source: U.S. Department of Labor, Bureau of Labor Statistics, Bulletin 1963, Employee Compensation in the Private Nonfarm Economy (Washington, D.C.: GPO, 1977), table 1, p. 8.

* Includes all direct payments to workers: straight-time pay; premium pay; paid leave, including sick leave; severance pay; and nonproduction bonuses.

† Includes employer expenditures for retirement programs; life insurance and health benefit programs (except sick leave); unemployment benefit programs (except severance pay); payments into vacation and holiday funds and into savings and thrift plans.

In addition to direct money payments, 8.1 percent of compensation for all private nonfarm employees in 1974 reflected employer expenditures for retirement programs, both legally required and private. Life insurance and health benefit programs accounted for 4.2 percent, and unemployment benefit programs, mainly legally required, for 1.1 percent.

Data available for manufacturing indicate that, at least for nonoffice workers, practically all of the growth in employer expenditures on supplements to direct wages has occured since the mid-1930s. Rees estimates that in 1935 supplements added, on the average, about half a cent per working hour to the compensation of production and related workers in manufacturing. This had increased to 3.5 cents by 1939, largely as a result of the enactment of federal social security legislation, and represented about 5.5 percent of total compensation.[9] In 1959, according to the Bureau of Labor Statistics survey data shown in Table 2.2, expenditures on supplements to direct wages for plant workers in manufacturing averaged 23 cents per working hour, or 8.6 percent of total compensation; by 1974, these figures had increased to 92 cents and 15.6 percent, respectively. The supplements proportion of total compensation increased steadily between 1959 and 1974.

Table 2.2. Factory Workers: Direct Wages and Wage Supplements as Proportions of Total Compensation per Hour Worked, 1959–74

Year	Total compensation per hour worked	Amount and percentage of total hourly compensation			
		Direct wages*		Supplement to wages†	
		Amount	Percent	Amount	Percent
1959	$2.61	$2.38	91.4	$0.23	8.6
1962	2.85	2.56	89.9	0.29	10.1
1966	3.30	2.93	88.8	0.37	11.2
1968	3.69	3.26	88.4	0.43	11.6
1970	4.24	3.70	87.4	0.53	12.6
1972	4.86	4.18	85.9	0.68	14.1
1974	5.88	4.96	84.4	0.92	15.6

Source: U.S. Department of Labor, Bureau of Labor Statistics, Bulletin 1963, *Employee Compensation in the Private Nonfarm Economy, 1974* (Washington, D.C.: GPO, 1977), table 39, p. 56.

* Includes all direct payments to workers: straight-time pay; premium pay; pay for time not worked, including paid sick leave; severance pay; and nonproduction bonuses.

† Employer expenditures for retirement programs; life and health benefit programs (except sick leave); unemployment benefit programs (except severance pay); payments into vacation and holiday funds and into savings and thrift plans.

There are a number of general observations that may be made about the structure of labor compensation as described above.

1. The figures shown in Table 2.1 (for the nonfarm economy) and Table 2.2 (for manufacturing) are broad averages. Actually, the relative importance of the elements of compensation vary substantially among industries and even, in many cases, among firms within individual industries. There is a distinct tendency for the

relative importance of pay supplements to vary directly with the level of compensation; that is, the higher the level of compensation the higher tends to be the proportion accounted for by employer expenditures for supplementary benefits. Thus, in establishments in the private nonfarm economy in which compensation for all employees in 1974 averaged less than $3.00 per hour worked, supplements accounted for 12.5 percent of total compensation; in establishments in which average compensation was between $9.00 and $9.99, supplements accounted for 27.1 percent of the total.[10] In general, the relative importance of supplementary benefits in the compensation package tends to be greater in large establishments than in small, and in union as compared with nonunion establishments. These factors tend of course to be highly correlated.

2. The introduction of new benefits and the liberalization of existing ones are alternatives, at least in part, to increases in basic rates of pay, and reflect in some sense worker preferences concerning the form that labor compensation should take. Particular wage settlements now typically, although not invariably, consist of some combination of changes in rates and benefits. The economic climate in which bargaining occurs tends to affect the two aspects of the wage bargain. In periods of rising prices, for example, major attention in most situations may focus on changes in rates of pay as workers seek to preserve their real living standards.

3. With respect to the direct money component of compensation, it is often useful to distinguish between rates, earnings, and take-home pay. Rates, as previously indicated, refer to pay for units of time or output. They anchor the wage structure. Earnings represent the yield of rates of pay, and may differ from expected earnings for standard hours of work because of short-time, on the one hand, or overtime, usually at premium rates, on the other. It should be noted, however, that an increasing proportion of the working population—about 14 percent in 1977—regularly worked on a part-time basis *by choice,* and hence their earnings would not correspond with the level expected of employees on standard hours.[11]

Few wage or salaried employees actually receive the full amount of their current earnings because of deductions for income and social security taxes, and, in many cases, for union dues, insurance, or other purposes. Gross earnings less deductions represent "take-home" pay,

11

the amount that the wage or salaried employee has available for current living expenses, other taxes, or for savings, and that he commonly perceives as his income from work. In a broader sense, of course, pay roll deductions—to the extent that they are not used for transfer payments—are for the most part a mechanism for the social provision of a variety of goods and services that contribute to living standards.

4. The fact that the wage bargain, in most instances, no longer can be described adequately in terms of basic rates of pay has a number of consequences that have received comparatively little notice. For example, the existence of complicated "packages" of rates and benefits must affect the cost of payroll administration. Again, some benefits (e.g., employer contributions for medical insurance or pension plans) have the advantage for workers of a form of compensation that does not add to taxable income.

Some supplementary benefits, particularly those related to length of service (e.g., nonvested pensions), may have a retarding effect on labor mobility. There is some evidence to suggest that unemployment insurance may serve to increase the average rate of unemployment.[12]

Money and Real Wages

The wage bargain is struck in terms of money, but money is an accounting convention. Real wages for a group of workers represent the bundle of goods and services they may purchase, on the average, with their money wages. Changes in real wages are obtained by dividing an appropriate index of rates of pay, earnings, or compensation by an index of consumer prices, each index relating to the same base period, and multiplying by 100. In the United States, of course, the Consumer Price Index prepared by the Bureau of Labor Statistics, although not strictly a cost-of-living index, typically is used to adjust money wage series for changes in living costs.[13]

It is important to notice that consumer price indexes throw no light on the standard of living that a given income can sustain, or on differences in living costs from one city or region in the country to another. For purposes such as these, data on the cost of one or more standard budgets are necessary.[14]

In terms of the wage bargain, workers seek generally to protect, and if possible to advance, the standard of life that their money wages or salaries afford. As discussed in some detail in Chapter 8, significant changes in the level of consumer prices, and expectations of future changes, constitute an important factor in money wage determination. For this purpose, of course, a widely accepted index of consumer prices is essential. Place-to-place differences in living costs, as measured by the costs of standard budgets, help in the interpretation of interarea wage rate differences, and may influence some other aspects of the wage bargain.

Suggested Readings

A useful discussion of supplementary or "fringe benefits" as an element of employee compensation will be found in Derek Robinson's *Wage Drift, Fringe Benefits, and Manpower* (Paris: Organization for Economic Cooperation and Development, 1968), chap. 3. See also Alvin Bauman's "Measuring Employee Compensation in U.S. Industry," *Monthly Labor Review,* October 1970.

3

Wages and the Labor Market

Whether viewed in terms of geography, occupations and industries, or size of labor force, the labor market in the United States is of awe-inspiring dimensions. The civilian labor force in 1978 averaged 100.4 million persons; employment averaged 94.4 million. The dynamism of the market is suggested by the shifting that constantly occurs in the allocation of this immense labor force among employments, industries, and areas, indicating a substantial measure of labor mobility.

Economic growth, the introduction of new products and services, changes in technology, and altered patterns of consumption affect the demand for workers; the dominant influences on the supply side are demographic and cultural. The most conspicuous demographic factor during the period since World War II has been the large influx of teenagers into the labor force beginning about the mid-1960s, a result of the baby boom of the immediate postwar years. The most significant cultural factors appear to be, first, the increased labor force participation rate of women, now at about 50 percent of those 16 years of age and over; and, second, a large increase in investment in "human capital" in the form of education and training, which in turn, and with some qualifications, appears to contribute to labor mobility.

Between 1970 and 1978, the labor force grew at an average annual rate of 2.5 percent—more than 2 million persons annually—substantially above the rate during the preceding 20 years. It seems likely that this rate will decline during the 1980s, with baby boom bulge and moderation of the recent increase participation rate. The participation rate of adult males, the higher age brackets, probably will continue to edge down, as it has since about the mid-1950s.[1]

Wages are determined within the confines of this large and complex market. And wages, as prices for the use of human effort in production, tend to respond, not promptly but certainly over periods of time, to forces affecting the demand and supply of particular categories of labor or of labor in general. This is not to say, however, that the "labor market" is equivalent to markets for commodities, or that the behavior of wages closely resembles that of most other prices. This decidedly is not the case. Wages cannot be explained fully by reference to market forces alone. The labor market has unique properties reflecting the human characteristics of the members of the labor force, and the relationships that develop between workers and employers.[2]

The Web of Custom and Social Relationships

In the determination of pay, notions of fairness and equity, especially when the pay of one job has been linked through custom with that of another, play a role in the pricing process. Long-established occupational wage differentials may be difficult to alter if they involve perceptions of fairness or status, even though an existing difference no longer conforms with underlying labor demand-supply conditions. Or, to give another example, the well known downward rigidity in the level of money wages, even when the labor market is loose and the level of other prices is falling, surely is related to the human tendency to resist reductions in accustomed levels of compensation. During the period following World War II, for reasons that are explored in a later chapter, the role of worker expectations with respect to upward wage adjustments appears to have assumed considerable importance.

Another factor conditioning pay determination is that relations between worker and employer vary widely from those between seller and buyer in commodity markets. Selling and buying in the markets for most goods and services usually involve little in the way of personal relationship. Most employment relationships, on the other hand, tend

15

to be of some duration, and to create conditions of mutual dependence and, in many instances, of loyalty.

In the employment relationship, the worker becomes habituated to the atmosphere, policies, and personnel of the firm for which he works, and these ties have been strengthened in recent decades by vacation, pension, and other benefits geared to length of service. For the employer, a competent worker who is familiar with the procedures of the enterprise, especially if he has acquired skills specific to his job, has a value over a new recruit who may need training and additional supervision.

The fact that labor effort in production is embodied in individuals clearly tends to impede, but certainly not eliminate, various forms of mobility that would facilitate adjustment to changes in demand-supply conditions in the labor market. Long ago Adam Smith, in comparing variations in wages in England and Scotland with variations in the prices of commodities, observed "that man is, of all sorts of luggage, the most difficult to be transported."[3] Workers do tend to develop strong attachments to particular places, occupations, firms, and industries. It is thus that they acquire identity and status. It is wrenching to change, when change involves the leaving of familiar surroundings, or the learning of new skills or tasks, or the adjustment to new work environments. It is well that this is so, for it lends a measure of stability to life generally and to business undertakings. Much would be lost if each employee were constantly on the lookout for some small wage advantage to be gained from transfer elsewhere, or employers were seeking constantly to secure small reductions in wage costs through the replacement of workers. Actually, it usually is sufficient at any particular time for only a small proportion of the work force to be mobile (and informed of alternative job opportunities) to bring about needed labor market adjustments.

The Roots of Trade Unionism

The fact that the employment relationship involves constant inter-action between worker and employer helps largely to explain the appeal to workers, especially in relatively large firms, of trade unionism as a labor market institution. The function of a business enterprise is to turn out products or services that consumers want to purchase at prices that will cover cost, including normal profit. Managerial decisions must be directed toward this end; otherwise, at least in the long run, the firm will cease to exist. These decisions involve a host of matters that affect directly the labor force of the enterprise, including wages, hours of work, safety, technological innovations, promotions, hiring practices, and procedures in the layoff and recall of workers. The personnel policies of a firm, and the administration of these policies, matter enormously in terms of employee well-being and capacity for work.

The basic function performed by trade unions is to provide a vehicle by which decisions directly affecting the welfare and status of workers are made jointly with management and not unilaterally by management. The invention that underlies the performance of this function is collective bargaining. The results of collective bargaining usually become embodied in agreements which, until their termination and for the subjects covered, provide standards of employment in the firms to which they relate. They provide a framework of rules, jointly determined, within which a great variety of day-to-day decisions affecting members of the work force can be made.

The cement that binds the ordinary worker to a union is mixed in the work place itself and is compounded of two elements: a sense of having participated, even though remotely, in decisions affecting the terms under which he is employed; and the knowledge, which usually is not remote at all, that he enjoys representation in day-to-day decisions relating to his employment status. A direct relationship tends to exist between the incidence of unionization and enterprise size. The main reason appears to be that in large firms the link between top management and the basic work force is at best highly attenuated, and the diffusion of managerial responsibility in matters of work rules and their administration often leads to questions of equity. The tendency in such situations is for workers to rely on collective rather than individual persuasion and strength to achieve "fairness" in wages, working rules, and their application.

In a perceptive analysis of theories of collective bargaining, Flanders argues "that the value of a trade union to its members lies less in its economic achievements than in its capacity to protect their dignity."[4] This is not to denigrate the economic role of unions, and specifically the part they play in the process of wage determination.

They frequently, though not always, exercise a measure of market power, in the sense that through collective bargaining levels of wages for organized workers are higher than labor market forces alone would dictate. And collectively bargained wage determinations may often exert an influence on wage changes in the nonunion sector of the economy. Unions are important also as vehicles for expressing the preferences of their members as to the way increases in compensation should be divided among the various components of the labor bargain.

But the wage objectives of even the most powerful unions are strongly constrained by labor market forces. Some attention is given in Chapter 9 to union-nonunion wage differences. Indeed, unions have not needed the advice of professional economists to develop or support policies calculated, from their perspective, to influence favorable developments in labor supply or demand. On the supply side, the long and ultimately successful union opposition to unrestricted immigration may be cited, and, for many of the skilled trades, restrictions on the ratio of apprentices to journeymen. With the great increase in the role of government in the economy, unions are now deeply concerned with governmental and some private policies that affect the demand for labor in general or in particular sectors of economic activity.

Governmental Intervention

In addition to collective bargaining as an institutional constraint upon the operation of purely market forces in wage determination, direct intervention in the wage-setting process by the federal government now occurs. Government wage policy takes two principal forms. The first involves the establishment of minimum wage standards in private industry, and, of lesser importance, of wage standards for workers in firms providing goods and services under contract with the government. The second relates to efforts during the period since World War II to influence the rate of increase in money wages through statutory or voluntary programs.

The federal Fair Labor Standards Act (1938) now provides basically for a uniform minimum wage for much of American industry. A series of laws, beginning in 1931, permits federal government determination of either prevailing or minimum wages that must be paid to the employees of contractors providing it with goods or services.

The setting of legal minimum wage standards for private industry generally represents a comparatively limited form of direct intervention by government in the wage determination process. It does serve, however, to anchor the wage structure, and, as we shall see in a later chapter, significantly affects the market impact on wages in some industries and areas. It has employment effects which are difficult to measure.

The second major element in federal wage policy is represented by episodic attempts to influence or control general wage (and price) behavior during the period following World War II. This effort reflects a search for ways to reconcile high level employment with reasonable price stability. It has been marked by statutory controls (1950–53) during the Korean war period; voluntary wage-price guideposts (1962–67); statutory controls again (1971–74); and a new voluntary guidepost program beginning in the fall of 1978.

Despite all the problems and difficulties, it seems probable that, in one form or another, some type of federal policy on the magnitude of wage adjustments will be with us for a long time. This likelihood has been increased by the prolonged inflation beginning in 1966. The winding down of this inflation involves, in part, diminishing the extent to which wage increases outstrip productivity gains and are factored into costs. Given the goals of high level employment and reasonable price stability, some kind of general "wage policy" almost inevitably will be part of a more comprehensive economic strategy where decision-making, as in wage determination, is widely diffused. At a minimum, persuasion will be used in attempts to dampen the exercise of market power over wage and price determination by unions and business firms.[5]

The Primacy of Market Forces

The factors discussed above impinge upon the operation of the labor market. Several other characteristics that help to distinguish the labor market from other types of markets deserve notice. One is that workers, even within particular occupations, are rarely perfect substitutes for one another. For example, sewing machine operatives in the garment industry, even in the same establishment, are not equally efficient, as indicated by sizable variations in incentive pay for the same operation. Not all professional economists or medical doctors are on the same level of proficiency. Worker selection procedures and wage payment methods seek at least in part to take these variations into account, and help to explain the dispersion of rates of pay that typically exists for given occupations within labor markets.

There is also the problem of labor market information. Workers do not have full information on alternative employment opportunities. Similarly, employers lack complete information with respect to the supply of labor or the exact margin to which it is profitable to increase or reduce employment with given changes in product markets or in wages or other costs. Moreover, there are costs for workers in job search (i.e., in the acquisition of information) and for the employers in the hiring and training of new employees.

Notably during the period since World War II, an extensive literature on the operation of the labor market has made its appearance. Submarkets for various types of labor have been identified, and the behavior of workers and employers within markets has been analyzed. Improvement in labor market efficiency has been sought since the 1930s by the development of a nationwide public employment service. An elaborate statistical system has been developed to throw light on the size, employment experience, and demographic characteristics of the labor force, and this system recently has been subject to intensive review.[6]

Information on the employment outlook for a large number of occupations, aimed especially at young people, is now regularly charted by the Bureau of Labor Statistics[7] and by some other organizations. Educational opportunities with a vocational orientation, and government-financed job training programs have multiplied. Job counseling in schools and other institutions has become widespread. Federal legislation now seeks to erase discriminatory practices believed to exist in a wide range of employments in the hiring and promotion of members of minority groups and women.

There has been a tendency in the literature to emphasize the imperfections in the operation of labor markets, stemming from obstacles to labor mobility and other factors. And, as we have seen, there are social and institutional elements that condition the behavior of wages. Yet wages contrive somehow to secure reasonably well allocations of labor among occupations and industries that conform in an approximate way to patterns of demand for output. If rates of pay did not tend toward the balancing of supply and demand for particular types of labor, then surpluses and shortages of labor of particular grades and skills would persist. This would lead to either controls on consumer spending or the deployment of labor by some central authority, or both. The disregard of market forces would lead at best to nonmarket efforts to shore up employment; indeed there are embryonic signs of this development in the United States in the use of public funds for "public service" job creation.

What often is not understood is that market forces, although they may require unpleasant and sometimes harsh decisions for individuals and firms, and create economic difficulties for communities, do serve to reconcile the freedom to spend, within the limits of one's income, and the freedom to work at the kind of job one prefers, within the limits of the available jobs for which one can qualify.

Lebergott has observed that in the United States "the labor market from 1832 to 1932 was, with a single qualification discussed below, as competitive as any in history."[8] The qualification, of course, was slavery, which was finally cast aside by the Emancipation Proclamation and the thirteenth amendment to the constitution. The market remains highly competitive, despite the growth of a number of institutional and governmental constraints since the 1930s.

Several concrete examples may serve at this point simply to suggest the power of the labor market. One is the sharp reduction over the past seventy years in the relative rates of pay of journeymen and helpers/laborers in the unionized building trades. This cannot be attributed to the pay policy of the construction unions, which are not noted for their egalitarian tendencies. It must reflect the changing evaluation in the labor market, as filtered through the collective bargaining process, of the relative rates of pay required to attract the supply of workers of varying skills demanded by the building industry.

A second example relates to the tremendous increase that has occurred during the period since World War II in the number of college-educated entrants to the labor force. During the seven-year period 1962–69, about 4 million graduates entered the labor force;

that number approximately doubled between 1969–76. As a consequence, competition sharpened for jobs in fields of work traditionally occupied by college graduates. A recent study reports that "although average salaries of newly hired graduates have risen since 1969, earnings of nongraduates have risen more rapidly. As a result, on average, the premium paid to college graudates has declined, both because competition in fields traditionally sought by graduates has kept salaries down and because relatively more graduates are in lower paying, nontraditional fields."[9]

The labor market, in a word, has to be looked upon as a complex phenomenon affected by a variety of conditions that ordinarily are not at work in markets for commodities or services to which it is tied through the production process. But it is a market through which wages (labor prices) are formed and labor is allocated among alternative uses. Adjustments within the labor market and its submarkets are affected by impediments that exist to labor mobility among occupations, industries, and geographic areas, and to the time required for such factor substitution as may be indicated by changes in the relative prices of labor and capital.

And yet the market does, on the whole, an effective job of deploying an enormous labor force in the production of the types and quantities of goods and services that consumers want to purchase. It has yielded over most of our history rising levels of real wages and living standards for the working population. Finally, it has provided the essential condition for freedom of choice of jobs within the bounds of those accessible. And that is a very great freedom indeed.

Suggested Readings

A concise and balanced treatment of the relative importance of social and market forces in wage determination will be found in E. H. Phelps Brown's *The Economics of Labor* (New Haven, Conn.: Yale University Press, 1962), chap. 5.

The nature of trade unionism as an institution is illuminated by Allan Flanders in "Collective Bargaining: A Theoretical Analysis," *British Journal of Industrial Relations,* March 1968. Reference should be made also to the seminal study by Selig Perlman, *A Theory of the Labor Movement* (New York: Macmillan, 1928), especially part 2, and to Milton Derber's *The American Idea of Industrial Democracy* (Urbana, Ill.: University of Illinois Press, 1970).

The background and development of governmental intervention in the labor market in the United States in the form of minimum wage legislation from 1912 to the passage in 1938 of the federal Fair Labor Standards Act is traced by Harry A. Millis and Royal E. Montgomery in, *Labor Progress and Some Basic Labor Problems* (New York: McGraw-Hill, 1938), pp. 301–75. Experience under the Fair Labor Standards Act is considered in chapter 10 of the present monograph.

For the post-World War II factors in government concern with wage-price policy, see *Exhortation and Controls: The Search for a Wage-Price Policy, 1945–1971* (Washington, D.C.: Brookings Institution, 1975), edited by Craufurd D. Goodwin.

4

The Occupational Wage Structure

Among its several meanings, the term "structure" implies a series of relationships. The wage structure of a plant or an office or, more broadly, of a national economy can be viewed as a series of wage rates designed to compensate workers for the varying skills and abilities required in the production process.

Wage rates usually are conceived as attached to occupations, each of which defines a particular type of work and the qualifications for its undertaking. For wage administration or other purposes, occupations at the plant level frequently are grouped into a limited number of labor grades, each consisting of a number of different jobs of approximately equal "worth" in terms of required training, education, effort, and other job characteristics. Especially for some kinds of analytical work, occupations often are divided into broad socio-economic classes, such as "professional," the precise classifications depending upon the problem at hand.

The concept of structure also has dimensional aspects. In the case of wages, the significant dimension is the number of workers at each rate in the scale. A wage structure is defined, therefore, not only by a series or hierarchy of rates, but also by the relative importance of each rate.

Whether for a particular plant or industry or for the whole economy, wage structures are subject to change through the operation of labor market forces. This chapter seeks to throw some light on the general structure of wages presently found in the United States, while the

24

following chapter deals with the broad changes that appear to have taken place in that structure over, roughly, the past 60 or 70 years.

Job Hierarchies

Modern industrial societies clearly require an immense range of labor skills. This gives rise to hierarchies of jobs within industries and across the economy. In general, the base of the hierarchy consists of a broad spectrum of routine manual and clerical jobs, although gradations of some significance in terms of required experience, training, and formal education are found even at this level. The apex of the pyramid consists of professional and higher level administrative and managerial jobs. Entrance to these occupations requires extensive formal training or experience, or both; additionally, continued effort typically is required to keep abreast of advances in basic knowledge, procedures, and technologies in the fields to which the jobs relate. In between is a broad band of occupations that embody craft or technical training or education of considerable dimensions, ranging from those in the skilled trades in such old industries as building or metalworking to technical occupations related to new industries such as electronics.

The modern labor force, in a word, is highly segmented by occupation. But jobs do not exist in airtight boxes. Even in the short run, movement of workers among jobs can and does occur. There are many essentially unskilled and semiskilled jobs among which considerable worker mobility exists over short periods.[1] These are types of work for which the training specific to particular jobs can be quickly acquired. For occupations that require extensive training or formal education, adjustment to changes in demand obviously is more difficult and prolonged.

Over the whole range of manufacturing and nonmanufacturing industry, literally thousands of occupations are identified in the *Dictionary of Occupational Titles* issued, primarily for job placement purposes, by the U.S. Department of Labor.[2] The most recent edition contains 21,741 defined jobs which are known by an additional 13,809 job titles. Many of these jobs are specific to particular industries; many others, such as arc welders, are found in a variety of industries; still others, such as typists (of various grades) occur across industry generally.

It is often useful for statistical or other purposes to group jobs into broad classes. For example, the Bureau of Labor Statistics identifies four major groupings to describe the occupational status of employed workers: (1) white-collar workers, including professional and technical, nonfarm managers and administrators, clerical, and sales workers; (2) blue-collar workers, including craft and kindred workers, machine operatives, except transport; transport equipment operatives, and nonfarm laborers; (3) service workers, including private household; and (4) farm workers. The United States Employment Service identifies nine major occupational groups in the classification scheme it has devised to facilitate its job placement work. The International Labor Office utilizes eight major categories to classify occupations for international comparative purposes.[3] The major groups, of course, typically are broken down into a variety of subgroups and these in turn into narrower job classifications.

The incredibly complicated occupational structure of modern societies presents a challenge to the analysis of the structure of pay. But just as it is useful to group occupations for insight into employment trends or for job placement, grouping also can be employed for pay purposes. This is possible because many jobs, although their specific duties differ, have similar composite scores in terms of required education or training, physical or mental effort, responsibility for materials and equipment, working conditions, and other job attributes. It is therefore possible to group jobs into limited numbers of grades or classes, and this is now widely done for pay administration purposes in both industry and government.

The essential problem is to determine in some fashion how dissimilar jobs should be ranked for pay purposes within a plant, office, or government agency. Jobs, of course, have always been ranked in some way. Historically, job ranking has been a rule-of-thumb process, and this is true to some extent today. On the basis of general knowledge, jobs at the lower and upper ends of the structure in a given employment complex usually can be spotted with reasonable accuracy. Then the employer or his representative places other jobs at various points in the scale. Often this is not even a highly conscious process. Many job and pay structures have developed and changed through numerous uncoordinated decisions. In the past, the process in many large establishments was often decentralized to department heads or even foremen.

There is nothing especially wrong with rule-of-thumb ranking if it works, in the sense of producing a pay structure that facilitates the recruitment and retention of workers for the jobs in the enterprise. It probably operates reasonably well in small establishments or where the structure of jobs is relatively simple. Its basic difficulty is that systematic consideration ordinarily is not and usually cannot be given to all of the major elements that go to make up a job. Almost by definition, there is no recourse to carefully prepared job descriptions. No clear procedure exists to take account of alterations in job requirements as products, methods, or technology change. Even though the structure may not break down entirely, constant patching is likely to be necessary, and grievances (either felt or expressed) over alleged inequities in classification may become a serious problem.

The rule-of-thumb approach to job ranking in a sense may be modified through collective bargaining. Bargaining over job classification may assume several forms. The union from time to time may appeal the appropriateness of particular classifications through an established grievance procedure. At the other extreme, management and the union may review the whole structure of jobs at one time. Job ranking influenced by bargaining may represent an improvement over the rule-of-thumb method in at least two ways. First, management may be forced to give greater thought to the problem of appropriate job relationships. Second, the union representatives may supplement the knowledge of job elements possessed by management. Collective bargaining, of course, is no guarantee that sound job structures will be established. Much depends on the attitudes of the parties and their willingness or ability to develop some sort of reasoned approach to job classification.

Since World War II, job evaluation as a technique for ranking jobs has developed remarkably, partly as an outgrowth of wartime pressure to rationalize wage structure in the aircraft, basic steel, and some other industries. Job evaluation may be defined as a systematic appraisal and ranking of jobs in terms of job requirements and working conditions. There are various systems of job evaluation. The present discussion is limited to the general nature of the process and to some of its advantages and limitations.[4]

Since job evaluation seeks to rank jobs in terms of their relative worth, ratings apply to jobs and not to the individuals who occupy them at the time of the evaluation. Successful evaluation is based on job

27

knowledge. The first step, therefore, is the preparation of detailed descriptions for at least the key jobs in the plant or other facility. These descriptions should include the job elements, such as skill, mental and physical effort, and working conditions, upon which evaluation will be based. The information contained in the descriptions is supplemented by the knowledge possessed by the evaluators. Ordinarily, jobs are appraised by a committee, which may consist of management representatives alone or of both management and employee members. Job evaluation as such is concerned solely with the ranking of jobs, and not with the wage rates that attach to the jobs.

In the rating process, an evaluation committee often will begin with several jobs that, by general consensus, fit into the lower and upper ends of the structure. Thorough discussion and agreement on the values to be assigned the factors for these jobs facilitate the rating of others. When all jobs are rated, they are then ranked (in point systems) according to their scores Jobs falling within a comparatively narrow range may be grouped for pay purposes. Thus, hundreds of jobs in a large plant may be slotted into a small number of labor grades or classes. The number of grades established will depend upon such considerations as the nature of the job requirements in the plant (primarily the range of skills required) and the nature of the wage system (i.e., whether flat rates or wide or narrow rate ranges are used).

Job evaluation is a technique for utilizing organized knowledge about occupations to arrive at informed and reasonably objective judgments as to the ranking of jobs. It is not, in any rigid sense, scientific. Judgment clearly enters into the evaluation process. Moreover, any particular job evaluation plan may fail to produce an acceptable ranking for some jobs. Exceptions, therefore, may have to be made, and these should be clearly recognized. Once established, the long-run value of a job evaluation plan depends upon the care and consistency with which it is administered, especially in the introduction of new jobs and the reappraisal of old jobs when their content changes. It can be a powerful tool of wage administration, materially reducing grievances relating to job classification and rates of pay.

A few examples of labor grade systems established through job evaluation will serve to illustrate the outcome of the evaluation process. The job-class structure in the steel-producing subsidiaries of the United States Steel Corporation, where the range of occupations is quite wide, presently consists of 34 labor grades. The upper grades (from about grade 21 on) are thinly populated, mainly by various categories of rollers, historically the aristocrats of the industry. Grades 15–17 contain many of the skilled crafts (carpenters, pipefitters, millwrights, bricklayers, etc.), together with many skilled jobs unique to steelmaking. Grades 1–3 consist of relatively unskilled laboring jobs. In the various grades in between are hundreds of jobs as evaluated jointly by representatives of management and of the United Steelworkers Union. As of August 1, 1976, the differential in average hourly rates of pay for nonincentive jobs (excluding cost-of-living allowances in effect on that date) between job classes 1–3, at the bottom of the skill ladder, and job classes 15–17, containing most of the skilled crafts, was about 31 percent.[5]

The plant labor force at Rockwell International (Electronics and North American Aircraft/Space Operations), under contract with the United Automobile Workers, was divided in 1976 into 18 labor grades for pay purposes. A range of rates was established for each grade, with automatic progression within each grade to the maximum rate. The differential in labor grade maxima, excluding cost-of-living allowances in effect but not incorporated into base rates, between labor grades 1–3 (janitors, garage attendants, and other relatively unskilled jobs) and labor grades 16–18 (tool and die makers, maintenance machinists, inspectors, major electronic systems, and many other highly skilled jobs) averaged 31 percent as of October 3, 1976.[6]

An example of a labor grade system relating to white-collar personnel may be found in the Lockheed-California Company, a major division of the Lockheed Aircraft Corporation. The employees in question are represented by the International Association of Machinists. In 1976, the hourly rated clerical and technical office force was slotted into 18 pay grades, each with a range of rates. As of October 2, 1976, the differential in average maximum rates for labor grades 16–18 (containing the lowest rated jobs) and grades 1–3 was 33 percent, again excluding cost-of-living allowances not incorporated into base rates.[7]

These examples of the results of labor grade systems arrived at through job evaluation are intended only to suggest how jobs may be grouped for pay purposes. They relate, of course, to specific complexes of jobs, two involving manual workers and the other white-collar personnel. They were chosen because the jobs involved embrace a wide range of skills in manual or nonsupervisory clerical and technical occupations. They were not selected as representative of "ideal" rankings of jobs, even in the industries to which they directly relate. They do indicate that large numbers of jobs, the specific duties of which differ significantly, can nevertheless be grouped for pay purposes on the basis of a number of general characteristics. It is upon these characteristics, presumably, that valuations for pay purposes are placed in the labor market.

As previously noted, the number of labor grades that a particular facility needs for wage structure purposes for, say, production workers, depends on a variety of factors. In many situations, 10 or 12 labor grades appear adequate; the number at United States Steel— 34— is unusually large. It might perhaps be pointed out that the approximately 1.3 million white-collar employees in the federal government's general pay system are classified into 18 grades. The occupations involved range from routine file clerks and messengers to the highest levels of professional and administrative work.

The National Structure of Pay

There is, of course, no evaluated structure for the major occupational groupings in the United States economy as a whole. That structure reflects the thousands of wage decisions that are made each year through collective bargaining or employer personnel administration. Nevertheless, considerable insight can be gained into the general structure of pay on the basis of wages for a few key jobs in major occupational groupings that are widely found across industry.

Unskilled and Skilled Manual Jobs

Table 4.1 shows straight-time average hourly earnings as of July 1975 for six relatively unskilled manual jobs and for six skilled maintenance jobs for all metropolitan areas combined in the United States. The level of hourly earnings at that time among the unskilled group ranged from $3.38 for janitors, porters, and cleaners (of whom about 29 percent were women, employed largely in nonmanufacturing industries) to $4.96 for power truckers (forklift), where the work force

Table 4.1. Selected Unskilled and Skilled Manual Occupations: Straight-time Average Hourly Earnings, United States, July 1975

Occupation	Straight-time hourly earnings			Coefficient of quartile variation (percent)	Index of mean rates (Laborers, material handling=100)
	Mean	Median	Middle range		
Unskilled					
Janitor, porters, and cleaners	$3.38	$3.19	$2.35–4.30	29	74.9
Laborers, material handling	4.51	4.42	3.41–5.56	24	100.0
Order fillers	4.46	4.35	3.30–5.56	26	98.9
Packers, shipping	3.98	3.84	3.00–4.75	23	88.2
Truckers, power (forklift)	4.96	4.99	4.09–5.94	18	110.0
Warehousemen	4.85	4.80	3.90–5.79	20	107.5
Skilled					
Carpenters, maintenance	6.14	6.10	5.31–6.94	13	136.1
Electricians, maintenance	6.44	6.54	5.60–7.41	14	142.8
Machinists, maintenance	6.25	6.38	5.50–6.99	12	138.6
Mechanics, general maintenance	6.00	5.99	5.15–6.85	14	133.0
Mechanics, automotive	6.32	6.58	5.55–7.21	13	140.0
Painters, maintenance	6.02	6.06	5.16–7.03	15	133.5

Source: U.S. Department of Labor, Bureau of Labor Statistics, Bulletin 1850–89, *Area Wage Surveys: Metropolitan Areas, United States, and Regional Summaries, 1975* (Washington, D.C.: GPO, 1977), table A-16, pp. 55–56, and table A-21, pp. 64–66.

was about 99 percent male and predominantly in manufacturing. Laborers, material handling, averaged $4.51. Among the skilled maintenance group of occupations, the range of average hourly earnings was comparatively narrow, from $6.00 for general maintenance mechanics to $6.44 for electricians.

Table 4.1 also shows for each occupation a simple measure of the absolute dispersion of rates of pay in the form of interquartile ranges; that is, the range of rates within which the middle half of the workers fall. Thus, the rates of pay in 1975 for the middle half of the material handling laborers fell between $3.41 and $5.56 an hour, a spread of $2.15. Among the skilled occupations, the interquartile range for electricians was $5.60–$7.41, a spread of $1.81 in hourly rates; among the other skilled jobs, the width of the middle range was greater than this only in the case of painters.

With minor exceptions, the absolute dispersion of rates of pay, as measured by the interquartile ranges, was greater for the unskilled than for the skilled occupations shown in Table 4.1. The difference in *relative* dispersion, as measured by the coefficient of quartile variation,* was consistently greater for the unskilled jobs. Thus, the coefficient for material handling laborers was 24 percent; for electricians, 14 percent. This suggests an important aspect of the American wage structure. To the extent that these jobs are representative of those at the lower and upper levels of skill for manual work, the market produces considerably greater variability in rates of pay for unskilled work.

The greater dispersion of rates of pay for the unskilled jobs undoubtedly reflects a variety of factors, including differences in the industrial distribution of the two groups of jobs. Thus, only about 43 percent of the workers in the unskilled jobs were in manufacturing industries, whereas almost three-fourths of the workers in the skilled maintenance occupations were employed in these industries. Industry differences also to some extent may reflect differences in job requirements and conditions of work even for the same general occupation. Thus, janitorial and cleaning work in a foundry differs considerably from that in an office building and may well influence the type of labor

---

* The coefficient of quartile variation is the ratio of the semi-interquartile range to the mid-quartile.

employed and the rate of pay. The work of order fillers or packers can vary substantially among plants and industries. The three jobs mentioned each employed a significant proportion of women (janitors, porters, and cleaners, 29 percent; order fillers, 19 percent; and packers, 36 percent). The proportion of women in the other unskilled jobs shown in Table 4.1, and in the skilled maintenance occupations, was very small.

If the level of earnings for material-handling laborers is designated as 100, then the average earnings of the other unskilled occupations, except for janitors, porters, and cleaners, fell within 12 percentage points, plus or minus, of this level. The average earnings of the six skilled occupations ranged from 33 percent to 43 percent above the level for laborers. The level of earnings for the skilled occupations as a group exceeded those for the unskilled jobs as a group (excluding janitors, porters, and cleaners) by about 35 percent. This general skill margin was about in line with that found in the evaluated job structures at United States Steel and Rockwell International described briefly in the preceding section. It must be emphasized, however, that pay margins for skill will differ, sometimes quite substantially, among individual production facilities and industries.

Nonsupervisory Office Jobs

Table 4.2 shows average earnings as of July 1975 for selected nonsupervisory office clerical jobs in the United States. The data are presented on an hourly basis to permit ready comparison with the levels of pay shown for manual occupations in Table 4.1. The range of average earnings within this group of clerical jobs was from $2.75 for file clerks, grade C, to $4.46 for accounting clerks, grade A. The average earnings of only 4 of 14 of the job classifications shown exceeded the average earnings of messengers ($3.17) by as much as 25 percent; in two instances, average earnings were below the messenger level.

Interquartile ranges again are presented as a simple indication of the dispersion of rates of pay in absolute terms, and relative dispersion is indicated by coefficients of quartile variation. Relatively, the dispersion of pay rates for these white-collar occupations is, on the whole, considerably smaller than for the unskilled manual jobs shown in

Table 4.2. Selected Office Clerical Occupations: Straight-time Average Hourly Earnings, United States, July 1975

Occupation	Straight-time hourly earnings*			Coefficient of quartile variation (percent)	Index of mean rates (Laborers, material handling=100)
	Mean	Median	Middle range		
Messengers	$3.17	$3.01	$2.63–3.53	15	70.3
Switchboard operators-receptionists	3.37	3.26	2.87–3.72	13	74.7
File clerks, A	3.87	3.64	3.14–4.36	16	85.8
File clerks, B	3.05	2.87	2.57–3.30	12	67.6
File clerks, C	2.75	2.62	2.39–2.99	11	58.1
Clerks, order	3.77	3.65	3.06–4.35	17	83.6
Clerks, payroll	4.03	3.84	3.29–4.56	16	89.4
Keypunch operators, A	4.04	3.87	3.46–4.42	12	89.6
Keypunch operators, B	3.49	3.33	2.95–3.83	13	77.4
Clerks, accounting, A	4.46	4.26	3.69–5.08	16	98.9
Clerks, accounting, B	3.49	3.33	2.91–3.86	14	77.4
Stenographers, general	3.82	3.67	3.19–4.32	15	81.4
Stenographers, senior	4.28	4.15	3.64–4.79	14	92.0
Typists, A	3.79	3.64	3.19–4.25	14	80.7
Typists, B	3.79	3.05	2.73–3.51	13	70.7

Source: U.S. Department of Labor, Bureau of Labor Statistics, Bulletin 1850-89, *Area Wage Surveys: Metropolitan Areas, United States, and Regional Summaries, 1975* (Washington, D.C.: GPO, 1977), table A, pp. 6–7.

* Average weekly salaries for standard work weeks divided by average standard hours.

Table 4.1, and is about in line with the coefficients for the skilled manual occupations.

It will be recalled that the straight-time average hourly earnings of material-handling laborers in July 1975 was $4.51. As the final column in Table 4.2 shows, this exceeded the level for each of the office jobs for which data are presented. Clearly there is a broad spectrum of white-collar employment in which average rates of pay are no greater than, and in some cases lower than, average rates for workers in relatively unskilled manual employments. The office jobs in question typically require a high school education and often the mastery of particular skills (e.g., shorthand dictation and typing in the case of stenographers or, in the case of accounting clerks, familiarity with office practices and procedures in the recording of accounting information). They are, for the most part, largely populated by women, which bears upon the supply of workers to such employments. And they differ from manual jobs in their distribution among industries, in working conditions, and in other ways.

Technical Jobs

Table 4.3 presents data on straight-time average hourly earnings for selected technical occupations as of July 1975. Such occupations typically require specialized study, usually at educational institutions, often supplemented by on-the-job training. For pay study purposes, as with some clerical jobs, the occupations shown in Table 4.3 are broken down into a number of grades, reflecting the difficulty of the duties performed and the degree of supervision received. To some extent, at least, lines of promotion must exist within these occupations based upon experience and perhaps additional training. Although these are essentially nonsupervisory jobs, occupants of the top grades may give direction and guidance to lower-grade employees.

With the exception of computer operator C and drafters C, the level of earnings in these jobs exceeded the level shown for all of the office clerical occupations in Table 4.2. The average earnings for the "A" grades, except for computer operators and industrial registered nurses, were above the levels for the skilled manual jobs for which data were presented in Table 4.1. Consequently, their earnings differentials over material handling laborers were higher, ranging from 48 percent

Table 4.3. Selected Technical Occupations: Straight-time Average Hourly Earnings, United States, July 1975

Occupation	Straight-time hourly earnings*			Coefficient of quartile variation (percent)	Index of mean rates (Laborers, material handling=100)
	Mean	Median	Middle range		
Computer operators, A	$5.58	$5.45	$4.81–6.15	12	123.7
Computer operators, B	4.69	4.50	4.01–5.18	13	104.0
Computer operators, C	3.96	3.81	3.36–4.40	13	87.8
Computer programmers, business, A	7.44	7.37	6.64–8.12	10	165.0
Computer programmers, business, B	6.17	6.04	5.33–6.88	13	136.8
Computer programmers, business, C	5.18	5.09	4.48–5.73	12	114.9
Computer systems analysts, business, A	9.15	8.97	8.12–10.09	11	202.9
Computer systems analysts, business, B	7.88	7.72	6.94–8.69	11	174.7
Computer systems analysts, business, C	6.87	6.64	5.82–7.83	15	152.3
Drafters, A	6.80	6.48	5.70–7.50	14	150.8
Drafters, B	5.41	5.25	4.66–6.03	13	120.0
Drafters, C	4.34	4.20	3.73–4.85	13	96.2
Electronics technicians, A	6.66	6.71	5.96–7.33	10	147.7
Electronics technicians, B	5.83	5.78	5.03–6.69	14	129.3
Electronics technicians, C	4.71	4.53	4.04–5.25	13	104.4
Nurses, industrial (registered)	5.58	5.46	4.84–6.23	13	123.7

Source: U.S. Department of Labor, Bureau of Labor Statistics, Bulletin 1850–89, *Area Wage Surveys: Metropolitan Areas, United States, and Regional Summaries, 1975* (Washington, D.C.: GPO, 1977), table A-6, pp. 28–30.
* Average weekly salaries for standard work weeks divided by average standard hours.

(electronic technicians A) to 103 percent (computer systems analysts A). The differential for computer operators A and for industrial nurses was about 24 percent. It will be recalled that the laborer/skilled maintenance worker differential ranged from approximately 34 to 43 percent.

The relative dispersion of rates of pay for the technical jobs, as indicated by the coefficients of quartile variation, correspond approximately with those shown for skilled maintenance jobs, and are narrower in most cases, although not markedly so, than for the office occupations. The relative dispersion ratios are decidedly narrower than those for unskilled manual jobs.

Professional and Administrative Jobs

Table 4.4 sets forth data on rates of pay and measures of salary rate dispersion as of March 1975 for a few professional occupations. As originally published, these salary data were on a monthly basis. They were reduced to hourly terms on the assumption of a standard 40-hour work week to facilitate comparison with the data previously shown for manual, clerical, and technical jobs.

As in the case of most of the technical jobs and several of the office clerical jobs, the professional and administrative occupations are divided into a number of grades or work levels for pay study purposes. For chemists and engineers, a classification is used which has eight grades; for attorneys and accountants, one with five.

For chemists, engineers, and accountants, the lowest grade is the entry level for professional work, and this typically requires a bachelor's degree or its equivalent in appropriate education and experience. Higher grades involve increasingly difficult work and usually supervisory duties of mounting responsibility. In the case of attorneys, the lowest grade again is at entry level, requiring a law degree plus admission to the bar. The work typically is of a relatively simple nature, with guidance given or available. In the higher grades, the work becomes more complex and substantively important, greater independence is exercised, and directing the work of other attorneys may become a significant job element.

In 1975, the average hourly rates of pay for entry-level chemists ($5.73) and engineers ($6.22) were above the levels for all of the

37

Table 4.4 Selected Professional Occupations: Average Hourly Salary Rates, United States, March 1975

Occupation	Average rate per hour*			Coefficient of quartile variation (percent)	Index of mean rates (Laborers, material handling=100)
	Mean	Median	Middle range		
Chemists, I	$5.73	$5.83	$5.31-6.23	8	127.1
Chemists, II	6.43	6.38	5.80-7.01	9	142.6
Chemists, III	7.62	7.59	6.83-8.37	10	169.0
Chemists, IV	9.30	9.19	8.36-10.24	10	206.2
Chemists, V	10.98	10.77	9.66-12.03	11	243.5
Chemists, VI	12.96	12.78	11.45-14.16	11	287.4
Chemists, VII	15.15	15.06	13.12-16.59	12	335.9
Chemists, VIII	18.27	17.96	15.43-20.19	13	405.1
Engineers, I	6.22	6.14	5.77-6.63	7	137.9
Engineers, II	6.87	6.75	6.29-7.36	8	152.3
Engineers, III	7.90	7.82	7.17-8.63	9	175.2
Engineers, IV	9.40	9.29	8.50-10.27	9	208.4
Engineers, V	10.82	10.70	9.81-11.77	9	239.9
Engineers, VI	12.60	12.43	11.25-13.73	10	279.4
Engineers, VII	14.02	13.70	12.30-15.40	11	310.9
Engineers, VIII	16.43	15.95	14.42-17.88	11	364.3
Attorneys, I	7.34	7.21	6.40-8.17	12	162.7
Attorneys, II	8.53	8.32	7.50-9.17	10	189.1
Attorneys, III	10.85	10.78	9.78-11.99	10	240.6
Attorneys, IV	13.56	13.27	11.97-14.99	11	300.7
Attorneys, V	16.37	16.03	14.30-18.27	12	363.0
Attorneys, VI	19.73	19.56	17.30-21.99	12	437.5
Accountants, I	5.23	5.19	4.64-5.71	12	116.0
Accountants, II	6.19	6.03	5.39-6.98	13	137.0
Accountants, III	7.02	6.85	6.14-7.73	11	157.0
Accountants, IV	8.49	8.32	7.63-9.23	9	188.0
Accountants, V	10.45	10.24	9.23-11.51	11	231.0

Source. U.S. Department of Labor, Bureau of Labor Statistics, Bulletin 1891, *National Survey of Professional, Administrative, Technical, and Clerical Pay, March 1975* (Washington, D.C.: GPO, 1975), table 2, pp. 14–15.

* Average salary rates per hour obtained by dividing average monthly salaries by 173.33 hours, on assumption of standard 40-hour work week.

clerical jobs shown in Table 4.2. With several exceptions they were below the highest levels shown for the technician jobs in Table 4.3. In several cases, the pay of workers in the lower technical grades (e.g., computer systems analysts) exceeded the rates for entry-level chemists, engineers, and accountants. The average rates of entry-level engineers were about in line with the average straight-time earnings for the skilled manual jobs in Table 4.1, but were lower for entry-level chemists and accountants. The average rates of entry-level attorneys were about the same as for the highest level of computer programmers, below the two highest grades for computer systems analysts, but above the level for skilled maintenance workers.

Normally, workers in professional occupations do not long remain in entry-level jobs. As they accumulate experience and years of service, they move up within their professions. How rapidly they move, and how far, depends on a number of factors, including their innate abilities, the extent to which they keep abreast of developments in their fields, their drive, and the size and nature of the organizations for which they work. It is interesting to note that the most heavily populated grade for both chemists and engineers is IV, with levels of hourly rates in 1975 of $9.30 and $9.40, respectively. This is marginally above the top level for computer systems analysts.

At the entry level, the differential in average earnings on an hourly basis between chemists and material-handling laborers was 27 percent; for engineers, 38 percent; for attorneys, 63 percent; for accountants, only 16 percent. These differentials widened, of course, for the progressively higher grade levels into which the professional occupations were divided. The rate levels for both chemists and attorneys in the top grades were in excess of four times the level for laborers; for engineers, more than three and a half times; and for accountants substantially more than double.

Table 4.4 indicates that the coefficients of salary dispersion for the professional occupations are relatively low; in fact, they are in general lower than for any other group of occupations that we have examined. Perhaps of particular interest are the coefficients for chemists and engineers. At the entry level, the coefficient of relative dispersion for chemists is only 8 percent and for engineers 7 percent. This seems to attest to the breadth and effectiveness of the market in the recruitment of college graduates with majors in these subjects. Beyond the entry level, the coefficients increase, but not strikingly so.

The entry-level coefficient for attorneys is considerably higher than for either chemists or engineers, but beyond that point there is little change in relative dispersion.

The General Shape of the Wage Structure

The limited data in the preceding pages should provide some insight into the general structure of wages in the United States. They give, of course, an extremely broad view, drawing on information for a few key occupations for metropolitan areas as a whole. Within these limits, however, data are shown for selected unskilled and skilled manual jobs, for a variety of nonsupervisory clerical employments, and for a number of technical and salaried professional occupations.

The jobs for which data are shown are found widely throughout industry. Except for general measures of wage dispersion, no effort has been made to deal with wage differences by industry, region, size of community, size of establishment, union status, method of wage payment, or other factors that have relevance for wage analysis.

And yet these data do provide a general view of occupational wage levels (as of 1975), and, more importantly, of their relationship for the great bulk of the nonfarm labor force in the United States. A broad summary statement would go somewhat as follows: in 1975, the federal statutory minimum wage was $2.10 an hour. Janitors (male and female), as Table 4.1 shows, had median earnings of $3.19 an hour, with one-fourth earning less than $2.35. The highest grade of engineer (the most numerous professional occupational group shown in Table 4.4) had median earnings of $15.95 an hour, with the upper one-fourth earning more than $17.88. It seems perfectly safe to say that in 1975 the rates of pay on an hourly basis of the overwhelming proportion of wage and salaried workers fell within these limits.

In an effort to obtain some notion of occupational wage relationships, the average (mean) hourly earnings shown for each occupation in the four tables in the preceding section was expressed as a relative of the average for material handling laborers. The earnings levels of the other unskilled manual jobs shown, except for janitors, were within about 12 percent of the average for laborers, while the levels for the skilled manual occupations were at least a third higher.

The earnings levels for the comparatively routine clerical jobs (Table 4.2) all fell below the level for laborers, in some cases by sizable percentages. These jobs are largely populated by women, but their relative standing in the wage structure is not in itself evidence of sex discrimination. It reflects a host of factors, including the supply of labor to such jobs, and differences in job requirements, working conditions, and employment among industries. It does point to a broad band of white-collar employment in which average rates of pay are, on the whole, lower than in relatively unskilled manual work.

With two exceptions, the level of earnings for the technical occupations (Table 4.3) was above the level for laborers, in most cases substantially. The average earnings of the three grades of computer systems analysts distinguished for salary survey purposes were 50 percent or more above the laborer level. In general, the level of salaries for most technical occupations appear to be at or above the average rates for skilled manual workers.

Entry-level engineers and chemists (Table 4.4) had average salaries, when computed on an hourly basis, roughly one-third above the laborer average. At the highest grade level for these two important professional occupations, average salaries were three and a half to four times the laborer average. The relative showing of salaried attorneys was better at all grade levels among the professional and administrative occupations shown. At the highest level, the average salary of attorneys was substantially more than four times as great as the laborer average.

Within all the occupations for which data are shown in the four tables, considerable dispersion of wage or salary rates is evident. In absolute terms, some indication of the extent of this dispersion is given by the interquartile (or middle) ranges. Relative dispersion is indicated by the coefficients of quartile variation. For the categories of jobs shown, relative dispersion was lowest for the professional occupations and greatest for the unskilled manual jobs. It was on the whole somewhat greater, but not markedly so, for the clerical jobs than for the skilled manual or technical groups.

It is doubtful if the rise in rates of pay since the mid-1970s has much altered this sweeping view of the contours of the wage structure in the United States. For wage relationships—for example, the differential in pay for skilled as against unskilled manual work—tend to change slowly. But these relationships are not fixed; they can and do change under the impact of powerful labor market and social and institutional forces. An effort is made in the following chapter to indicate something of what has happened to the pay structure during the present century.

Suggested Readings

Analyses of the national occupational wage structure are not numerous, but see Albert Rees's *The Economics of Work and Pay* (New York: Harper & Row, 1973), chap. ll, and Melvin W. Reder's "Wage Differences: Theory and Measurement," in National Bureau of Economic Research, *Aspects of Labor Economics* (Princeton, N.J.: Princeton University Press, 1962), especially pp. 257–76.

A brief but particularly clear description and appraisal of job evaluation remains that of E. R. Livernash, "Job Evaluation," in W. S. Woytinsky and associates' *Employment and Wages in the United States* (New York: Twentieth Century Fund, 1953), chap. 35.

5

The Trend of Occupational Wage Differentials

The question of whether, and of the extent to which, change has occurred in the present structure of pay is of considerable interest. Have differentials in pay for skilled as against unskilled manual workers increased or diminished? Has change occurred in the relative position of professional workers in the wage and salary structure? In more general terms, has there been a reduction in inequality of pay for the working population?

At least for the twentieth century, the evidence on this question for manual occupations can be approached with some confidence. For other major occupational groups, the required data over an extended period are not abundant. Some clues are available, however, as indicated below.

Such changes as have occurred in relative wages among occupations reflect the complex interaction of labor market forces, including the institutional arrangements that play a role in wage determination and administration. These changes should be interpreted as applying to major occupational groups, and not necessarily to each specific occupation within broad categories of jobs.

Some Evidence on Change in Skill Margins

Manual Occupations

One of the striking characteristics of the wage structure for manual workers in the United States has been the tendency for occupational wage differentials to narrow during the twentieth century. This tendency was first documented in a pioneering study by Ober of skill margins for manual workers in factory employment during the period 1907–47.[1]

For the purpose of measuring the trend in occupational pay differences in manufacturing, Ober used the spread between rates for unskilled and skilled labor. He pointed out that these extremes of the occupational rate structure define the limits of the spread within which all other rates for manual workers are found, and that, consequently, a narrowing of the spread between skilled and unskilled rates reflected a narrowing of differentials among all occupations. Ober's analysis for factory workers related to five periods between 1907 and 1947, and the study, using a somewhat different methodology,[2] has been extended to 1976 by the Bureau of Labor Statistics.

Table 5.1 shows the percentage by which, on the average, the earnings of skilled factory workers exceeded the earnings of unskilled at various periods between 1907 and 1976. In 1907, the average earnings of skilled factory workers were more than double those of the unskilled; this difference had fallen to 75 percent by the end of World War I. There was a small rise in the average differential between 1918–19 and 1931–32. A fairly marked decline (to 65 percent) occurred during the latter part of the 1930s, and a further decline to 55 percent by the end of World War II. By 1953, at the end of the Korean War, the average differential had fallen to 37 percent. It remained comparatively stable thereafter to 1967, but experienced a further decline to 31 percent by 1976.

Table 5.2 shows cents-per-hour as well as percentage differences in average union wage scales between journeymen and laborers/helpers in the building trades for selected years between 1907 and 1978. The decline in the relative differential roughly paralleled the decline in the skilled-unskilled ratio in manufacturing. In the case of the building trades, the drop was particularly sharp between 1937–40 and the immediate post-World War II period. The differential continued to decline and by 1967 the average union rate for the skilled crafts was only 32 percent above the average rate for laborers/helpers. Thereafter, to 1978, the skill margin in building remained stable.

In money terms, the skilled-unskilled differential in the building trades widened consistently during this period of decline in the

Table 5.1. Relationship between Average Hourly Earnings of Skilled and Unskilled Workers in Manufacturing, 1907–76

Date	Percentage by which average hourly earnings of skilled workers exceeded average for unskilled
1907	105
1918–19	75
1931–32	80
1937–40	65
1945–47	55
1953	37
1956	38
1962	36
1967	36
1976	31

Source: Harry Ober, "Occupational Wage Differentials, 1907–47," Monthly Labor Review, August 1948, p. 130; for 1953 and 1956, U.S. Department of Labor, Bureau of Labor Statistics, Bulletin 1575–87, Wages and Related Benefits, part 2: Metropolitan Areas, United States and Regional Summaries, 1967–68 (Washington, D.C.: GPO, 1969), p. 79; for 1962, 1967, and 1976, estimates supplied by Bureau of Labor Statistics.

relative differential. It is probable that the same development occurred in manufacturing. The acceptance by skilled workers of a decline in their wage position and living standards relative to those of unskilled workers undoubtedly was made easier, or was at least masked, by the increase in the differential in absolute or money terms. As suggested at a later point in this section, there appear to be limits to the compression of relative pay differentials, and these limits, at least temporarily seem to have been reached by the early 1950s in manufacturing. In building, the compression of relative wage scales continued into the 1960s.

The fact must be emphasized that we have been dealing with average skill margins in manufacturing and the building trades. Among individual industries, the margin between rates of pay for skilled and unskilled work varies considerably. For 1967, the Bureau of Labor Statistics computed the differences between rates of pay for janitors and for seven selected skilled occupations in 36 manufacturing industries in metropolitan areas. Maintenance electricians may be used as an example. In 10 of the 36 industries, the skill margin for this occupation fell below 35 percent; in 15 industries, between 35 and 45 percent; and in 11 industries, the margin exceeded 45 percent.[3]

The same Bureau of Labor Statistics study also indicated that in 1967 average skill margins for manual workers tended, with some

Table 5.2. Relationship between Average Union Wage Scales* for Journeymen and Laborers/Helpers, Building Trades, Selected Periods, 1907–78

Date	Percentage by which average wage scales for journeymen exceeded averages for laborers/helpers	Average cents-per-hour difference between wage scales for journeymen and laborers/helpers
1907	76	$0.21
1916	112	0.29
1918–19	93	0.33
1920–21	77	0.44
1931–32	90	0.61
1937–40	81	0.62
1945–47	57	0.66
1953	44	0.88
1956	40	0.92
1962	34	1.06
1967	32	1.24
1974	32	2.14
1978	32	2.76

Source: Arthur Rose, "Wage Differentials in the Building Trades," *Monthly Labor Review,* October 1969, pp. 14–17, for 1907–67; extension to 1978 by the author.

* To minimize the effect on published average rates of membership shifts from year to year, standardized wage scales were developed for the journeymen crafts and for the laborers/helpers classifications.

exceptions, to be greater in broad nonmanufacturing industry groups than in manufacturing. Estimates for nonmanufacturing as a whole for 1976 show that this tendency still exists. One reason is that the wages of unskilled workers in many nonmanufacturing industries—e.g., retail trade—tend to be below manufacturing levels, while wages in the skilled trades are often higher. In some nonmanufacturing industries, however, skill margins in 1967 were quite narrow, notably on the railroads and in local urban transportation. Attention has already been directed to the building industry.

Why has a secular decline occurred in occupational wage differentials for manual work? Reder has offered a provocative theoretical explanation.[4] The available evidence indicates that skill margins have declined most decisively during periods, such as the two world wars, of exceptional tightness in the labor market. In summary terms, Reder argues that when labor markets are exceedingly tight employers tend to substitute less skilled workers for those who are more skilled, or alter production processes to facilitate the use of less skilled workers, or both, rather than simply to bid up wage rates. This process of substitution affects workers at various levels of skill within enterprises, and, in effect, is a source of increased labor supply above the unskilled level. But this process cannot operate at the least skilled level, assuming full employment and a fixed labor force. Hence, when the unemployed have been absorbed, employers are faced with a reduced supply of unskilled workers and therefore tend to drive up wage rates for this type of labor relative to those for workers in more skilled jobs. Reder's basic hypothesis is that " . . . the association of short-period variations in skill margins with the level of aggregate employment is due to the fact that a rise in the level of employment for all grades of labor reduces the supply of labor available for unskilled jobs (at initial wage rates) proportionately more than it reduces the supply available for others."[5]

The reduction of skill margins during boom periods does not necessarily mean that margins will widen when labor markets loosen. This did in fact happen during the sharp but short-lived depression following World War I, but not during the prolonged depression of the 1930s. To explain this phenomenon, Reder develops the concept of a "social minimum wage," which may be set by statute, social custom, or trade union policy, or some combination of these, and is related also, at least indirectly, to the assistance that wage earners may obtain from social security, welfare programs, and other sources. It places a floor under the wage rate that a worker need or will accept in private or public employment. In Reder's view, the rates of pay for unskilled work during the depression that followed World War I were generally above the social minimum wage, and hence wage reductions in response to market forces were not inhibited. By 1929, however, the social minimum had more or less caught up with the prevailing wage rates for unskilled labor, and hence the skill margins did not widen during the catastrophic downturn in economic activity that occurred between 1929 and 1933. Between 1933 and 1940, Reder credits a further upward shift in the social minimum wage, due to New Deal legislation and the general social climate, for the narrowing of skill margins that evidently occurred during that period of continuing high unemployment.

Reder's analysis throws light on important aspects of the behavior of skill margins for manual work during the present century. His analysis of employer adaptation to tight labor markets, and of the "social minimum wage" in relation to the reserve price of labor, is illuminating. However, a number of underlying factors affecting the labor market during the period with which we are concerned deserve emphasis in any consideration of the secular course of skill margins.

The first of these factors is the sharp decline in immigration that occurred during World War I and the subsequent change in immigration policy, which reduced drastically the net inflow of population from abroad. For the five-year period ending June 30, 1914, the excess of immigrants over emigrants was 3,733,000. About three-fourths of the economically active immigrants during this period were classified as laborers (except farm and mine), farm laborers, service workers, and private household workers.

Immigration restriction, which had long been urged by dominant sections of the labor movement, served to decrease the rate of labor supply growth. This effect of curtailed immigration was reinforced by a declining birth rate until the latter half of the 1940s. These two developments tended to ease the pressure of labor supply on employment opportunities generally, but especially on jobs at the relatively unskilled level.

Another development served to augment the supply of workers for skilled manual jobs and for the expanding segment of white-collar employment. This was the extension, both legally and in terms of social custom, of the school-leaving age. In 1920, 50.8 percent of those 16 years of age were attending school. This percentage had increased to 66.3 by 1930, 76.2 by 1940, and 82.0 by 1950. The proportion of 18-year olds in school increased from 21.7 percent in 1920 to 41.2 percent in 1950. Entrance into the full-time work force was thus delayed for larger and larger proportions of young people. Greater occupational choice accompanied the increase in formal education, including training in vocational and technical subjects. More skilled and better-paying jobs, including those in the expanding nonmanual occupational categories, thus became accessible to larger proportions of workers.

Yet another development blended with the underlying labor supply factors outlined above. Gradually and almost unnoticed, a technical revolution occurred in large areas of unskilled work. The "unskilled laborer" became a man with mechanical equipment. Excavating, loading and unloading, stacking—these areas of heavy labor became substantially mechanized. Mechanical devices were brought even to the aid of the janitor and charwoman. In substance, the productiveness of unskilled labor was enhanced through combination with larger quantities of capital. The shift from the exercise of sheer manual power, aided at best by hand tools, to the use of power equipment caused many jobs to become, in a sense, less unskilled. "Common labor" tended to be broken down into separate jobs with specific job titles.

The broad effect of these various factors on the labor market was to decrease the supply of unskilled relative to skilled and semiskilled labor. On this basis, in a generally expanding economy, one would expect a gradual contraction of skill margins. Other factors evidently were at work, however, in the sharp declines that occurred over short periods during the exceedingly tight labor markets that characterized the two world wars. Part of the explanation surely is found in Reder's perceptive analysis, described earlier, of the upgrading and hiring practices of firms during such periods. But another factor also played a role of some significance; namely, a tendency to grant increases in money wages predominantly across the board in uniform cents per hour, which meant larger increases in percentage terms for the lower-paid workers. This tendency was plainly evident during World War II and the years roughly to 1953, and had its roots in both government and trade union wage policy.[6] It undoubtedly was related to the inflationary situation that existed, with one interruption, during this period.[7]

With respect to government wage policy during World War II, the National War Labor Board, in its wage stabilization program, held that allowable general increases must be granted uniformly in cents per hour. This policy was adopted deliberately under the so-called Little Steel Formula in the interest of low-paid workers. The National Wage Stabilization Board, which functioned from January 1, 1946, to February 24, 1947, sancationed wage increases that were "consistent with the general pattern of wage or salary adjustments" established in an industry or local labor market between August 18, 1945, and February 14, 1946. In this period, government wage control policy largely conformed with the terms of private wage bargains. These bargains were heavily influenced by the wage recommendations of government fact-finding boards, which functioned in a number of important labor-management disputes in the immediate postwar era. Their recommendations typically were couched in cents per hour terms.[8]

In the Korean emergency (1950–53), government wage stabilization policy placed no restrictions on the way in which allowable general wage increases could be distributed. But its policy was organized around cost-of-living wage escalation, and such adjustments, at least under formal escalator arrangements in collective bargaining agreements, typically provided for increases across the board in cents per hour terms.

The conjuncture of government and union wage policy during World War II and through the Korean War reflected the inflation that began to manifest itself in early 1941, continued into the immediate post-World War II years, and, after a brief respite in 1948–49, flared up again during the Korean emergency. There was a marked tendency for unions, beginning in 1941, to formulate their wage demands in terms of uniform money increases and for settlements to be made in that fashion.

There were at least two reasons for this development. The first is that wage increases in an inflationary period are designed largely to offset increases in living costs. Lower-paid workers tend to spend a larger proportion of their incomes than higher-paid workers for basic cost-of-living items, such as food. Hence they may, depending on relative price movements, experience higher than average increases in living costs. Uniform money wage increases, which are larger for lower-paid workers in percentage terms, may therefore appear more equitable than differential increases.

The second reason is that it is politically easier in an inflationary period for union leadership to press for uniform money increases. All workers thus appear to be treated equally. In industrial or quasi-industrial unions, unskilled and semiskilled workers typically make up a substantial majority of the membership. Their political power within the union is bound to be an important consideration in formulating demands and in bargaining strategy. Under these circumstances, only a strongly disciplined union with a well-articulated wage structure policy can agree readily to differential money increases. As suggested earlier, skilled workers, within limits, may be content with the maintenance of absolute wage differentials, even though their relative wage position is deteriorating. This is even more likely to be the case if, as in the building trades, absolute differentials widen while relative differentials contract.

Occupational wage differentials among manual workers in manufacturing appear to have stabilized for at least two decades after 1953. Indeed, special wage adjustments for skilled workers were made in that year in the automobile, electrical machinery and equipment, radio, and other industries, as considerable unrest among skilled workers began to surface. This unrest may have reflected a dissipation of the "money illusion"; that is, that preservation of differentials in money terms maintained relative wage standards. In any event, inflation, which appears to have been a factor in declining relative wages, was arrested; in fact, consumer prices over the 12 years from 1953 to 1965 increased at an average annual rate of only 1.4 percent. Another factor during this period may well have reflected the large shift of workers out of agriculture into urban employments, which probably augmented the relatively unskilled labor supply. In industry generally, more attention began to be given to the improvement and administration of wage structures,[9] and the distribution of general pay increases was less likely to be made uniformly in money terms.

Beginning in 1966, inflation again became an important factor in the determination of money wages, and as of this writing (1979) has persisted for more than a decade. With respect to government wage policy during this period, a program of mandatory wage controls (1971–74, in four phases) was designed to permit wage administrators to "handle problems of wage structure within the guideline [to wage increases] as they saw fit."[10] However, in the application of the guideline, higher increases were permitted to low-wage workers to bring their wages up to a specified standard,[11] and this, in conjunction with statutory minimum wage increases during this period, may have had some narrowing effect on relative pay differences. A marked increase in cost-of-living escalator provisions in union agreements also occurred. Aside from formal escalation arrangements, which cover a comparatively small proportion of the labor force, inflation may affect the distribution of wage increases much more generally, with relatively higher increases awarded to lower-paid workers.

The conclusion of this discussion of the trend over the past seventy years of pay differentials for manual jobs is that underlying labor market conditions gradually would have produced a narrowing of relative pay differences. The sharp contractions in skill margins that occurred in several comparatively brief periods was associated with extraordinarily tight wartime labor markets and with inflation. By the mid-1950s, the contraction of skill margins in manufacturing had led to unrest among skilled workers in a variety of industries and substantially to the stabilization of the average margin, at least until the 1970s.

There is, of course, no unalterably "correct" structure of wage differentials for a firm or industry; the structure will change as demand-supply conditions in the labor market change. In the short run, job rate differentials need be no greater than are necessary to retain the kinds of labor needed by the firm. In the long run, however, the use of differentials to induce training and the responsibility that goes with higher-level jobs cannot be neglected.

The consideration thus far of the trend of occupational wage differentials has related to manual jobs. Unfortunately, data that would permit the extension of this analysis to clerical and higher-level white-collar occupations are fragmentary and unsatisfactory. However, some observations may be advanced with reference particularly to clerical and professional employments.

Clerical Occupations

Well over a century ago John Stuart Mill, with British conditions in mind, wrote that the differential in pay between employments that required "even the humble education of reading and writing" and those of "ordinary labor" had "greatly fallen" through the spread of elementary education, which had largely increased competition in the clerical labor market. He believed, however, that the differential in pay between clerks and laborers was still too great, partly because education was not yet "so generally diffused as to call forth the natural number of competitors," and partly to the persistence of custom that prescribed higher standards of dress and appearance to clerical employees.[12]

Since Mill wrote, immense advances have occurred in the supply of workers to clerical and other types of white-collar employment below the technical and professional job levels. The supply of workers to such employments reflects not only advances in the educational attainment of the work force, but significant changes in its composition. With respect to the latter, the increased labor force participation rate of women is particularly noteworthy. As indicated in Chapter 3, that rate by the end of the 1970s had reached about 50 percent of the women 16 years of age and over. This influx greatly augmented the supply of workers to most clerical jobs and to many technical and quasi-professional occupations as well.

This increase in supply has been countered by large increases in demand for workers for a broad range of clerical and other types of white-collar jobs below the professional level. This reflects, of course, the great shifts that have taken place in technology and in the character of output in the American economy.

Unfortunately, data are not available that would permit confident measurement over some extended period of pay for clerical occupations in relation to pay for manual jobs. For the short period from 1960 to 1973, the average salaries of office clerical workers in metropolitan areas increased by 74.1 percent, compared with an increase of 85.4 percent for unskilled plant workers and 82.7 percent for skilled maintenance workers.[13] In the mid-1970s, as shown in Chapter 4, average rates of pay in a range of office clerical jobs were lower than the average pay for material-handling laborers.

Professional Occupations

We can draw upon the work of Scitovsky for some insight into the course of relative earnings in professional occupations.[14] For various periods ending in 1958, Scitovsky noted a general decline in average earnings for five professional occupations in relation to the per capita income of the gainfully occupied population in the United States and in selected foreign countries. For the United States, the trend among the five occupations was not consistent. As multiples of the per capita income of the gainfully occupied, the average earnings of lawyers, professors, and higher civil servants declined between 1929–30 and 1958. On the other hand, the relative position of physicians improved markedly and of dentists to a lesser extent. With respect to physicians, Scitovsky notes that their number per 100,000 of the population had been declining at least since 1900. Since 1958, however, the physician-population ratio has improved, but this increase in supply probably has been more than offset by an increase in demand for medical services arising from the growth of real income, private medical insurance, and government programs for financing health care for some segments of the population.

Scitovsky points to a number of factors affecting, in general, the income position of the professions in modern industrial societies. Not all of these operate in the same direction. In his view, the most important factor tending to increase the supply of workers to professional occupations "is the increasing availability of higher education and its diminishing cost to the individual."[15] To a limited extent, this factor has been offset by rising educational requirements for eligibility to the professions. But while the supply of professional services has been increasing, so has the demand for such services as a consequence of the growth of real incomes. Moreover, the increasing complexity of present-day society has created a demand for new professions and occupations that require extensive scientific and technical training. The new occupations compete with the older professions for the available supply of highly educated and trained manpower. These two factors—the growth in real income and the rise of new professional occupations—has cushioned the income depressing effect of the increase in the supply of professional personnel. Scitovsky notes a third factor in the demand equation, one that is likely to have a downward influence. This is the probable lag in the productivity of professional personnel, which tends to raise the prices of their services relative to the prices of most other goods and services.

Finally, there is the factor of inflation. Scitovsky is inclined to believe that professional incomes are determined to some extent by tradition, and "respond sluggishly to market forces and may have a range of indeterminacy within which they do not respond at all."[16] Especially during periods of small rises in prices or at the beginning of a more severe inflationary episode, the salaries or fees of professional workers may lag. In a prolonged inflation, however, professional incomes may be as well protected by market forces through upward adjustment as the incomes of other groups. However, if these incomes exceed the level justified by underlying supply-demand conditions, inflation may provide a correction through the reduction in real terms of professional salary scales and fees.

The professions, as suggested by Scitovsky's data, are not uniform in their salary or income behavior. Over the long term, incomes in professional occupations, as a group, appear to have declined relative to those for occupations requiring lesser training and skill. But their movement, certainly within short periods, can be diverse. Two examples, using recent date, will suffice. Thus, the salaries of public school teachers rose more sharply than the rates of pay of production and nonsupervisory workers in private nonfarm employment between 1953 and 1971.[17] This was a period of strong demand for teachers to meet the increased school enrollment resulting from the "baby boom" of the immediate postwar years. The output of teachers, with an obvious lag, responded to this increase in demand, and by the mid-1970s the market for teaching positions in the public schools had become quite competitive. Enrollment in elementary schools peaked in 1967 and in high schools in the early 1970s. Since 1971, the rate of increase in teacher salaries has fallen slightly behind the rise in rates of pay for production and other nonsupervisory workers in the private economy. Over the comparatively long period from 1925 to 1978, the pay differential between public school teachers and industrial workers appears, on the basis of crude estimates, to have narrowed substantially.[18]

The second example relates to positions in the higher grades in the federal white-collar civil service, where salaries had so deteriorated, relatively, by the early 1960s that severe problems of recruitment and retention were being encountered. Between 1939 and June 1962, prior to the passage of the Federal Salary Reform Act of that year, the entrance salary for grade 15 in the Federal service had increased by only 71.6 percent, a decline in real terms of 21.1 percent. This was far less than the increase in private salaries generally, and less, by varying amounts, than increases to lower civil service grades. The Salary Reform Act, linking Federal government salaries to those in private industry, provided the basis for substantial differential increases in pay to the higher civil service grades.[19]

Skill Margins and the Labor Market

The more one reflects on the course of occupational wage differentials or skill margins, the more one is impressed by the strong currents that operate in the labor market. During the twentieth century, major factors on the supply side have been the curtailment of immigration, which affected particularly the influx of relatively unskilled workers; the extension of opportunities for secondary, technical, and advanced education; the large post-World War II shift of workers out of agriculture; and, since the 1950s, the steady increase in the labor force participation rate of women. Other noteworthy developments include the breaching of barriers to areas of employment from which blacks, some other minorities, and women had been largely excluded by prejudice or tradition.

On the labor demand side, the economy expanded remarkably despite the great depression of the 1930s and lesser recessions. Between 1900 and 1978, gross national product in real terms increased at an average annual rate of about 3 percent. Whole new industries made their appearance. Technological innovations, large and small, had enormous impact on the character of output, productivity, job requirements, and job opportunities.

Total civilian employment (16 years of age and over) in 1978 averaged 94.4 million, as compared with 46.1 million (14 years of age and over) in 1929, and about 27 million in 1900 (the respective unemployment rates were 6.0 percent in 1978, 3.2 percent in 1929, and 5.0 percent in 1900). Within this large change in the total volume of employment, there was a vast shift in its composition. Employment in white-collar jobs increased not only absolutely but relative to employment in blue-collar occupations. Within each of these broad categories, the configuration of education, training, experience, and other job attributes required of the work force altered under the impact of changes in the character of output and of advances in knowledge and technology, not all of which operated in the same direction. That the labor market, with all its imperfections, was able reasonably well to adjust labor supply to demand in this dynamic context is a tribute to its power.

In the process, as we have seen, a general contraction of occupational wage differentials appears to have occurred since the beginning of the century. This contraction reflects long-term labor market developments, but was accelerated or retarded over short periods by special conditions or forces. The evidence must be interpreted as relating to broad occupational groups. Not all individual occupations were equally affected.

This development was not peculiar to the United States, as shown by a broad survey by Phelps Brown of change in the structure of pay in a number of industrial countries. He remarks that we have noticed few differentials that have widened in the course of time, and many that have contracted. The contemporary changes that would account for this include the extension of education and the rise in the standard of living, reducing the differences of mental and physical capability between one person and another; the increased quantity and ingenuity of equipment, reducing dependence on the skill of the worker and increasing the productivity of the less skilled; but also the increased unionization of the less skilled; and the policy of governments, and in some times and places of trade unionism, seeking to raise the lowest-paid or maintain a social minimum.[20]

Suggested Readings

In an original investigation, "Long-Run Changes in Occupational Wage Structure, 1900–1956," *Journal of Political Economy,* December 1960, Paul G. Keat generally confirms previous findings and suggests forces affecting relative wage differentials. See also Lloyd G. Reynolds and Cynthia Taft's *The Evolution of Wage Structure* (New Haven, Conn.: Yale University Press, 1956), chap. 12, especially pp. 316–27, and chap. 13. Alan L. Gustman and Martin Segal, in "The Skilled-Unskilled Wage Differential in Construction," *Industrial and Labor Relations Review,* January 1974, advance an explanation for the narrowing of skill margins during 1953–70. A broad survey of change in wage and salary structure in a number of countries, including the United States, is presented by Henry Phelps Brown in *The Inequality of Pay* (Berkeley and Los Angeles: University of California Press, 1977), chap. 3. Robert Ozanne, in "A Century of Occupational Differentials in Manufacturing," *Review of Economics and Statistics,* August 1962, questions the view presented in previous research and accepted here of the long-term trend of skill margins in factory employment.

6

Wage Dispersion within Occupations

In the preceding two chapters, wage structure was considered largely in terms of average wages or salaries for occupations selected to represent major categories of employment in urban areas, and with change in occupational pay differentials. A simple measure of dispersion was attached to the occupational averages shown in Chapter 4. We now want to look more closely at differences in rates of pay within occupations, and suggest some of the reasons for the observed dispersion.

In any substantial labor market, a considerable dispersion of rates of pay will exist for a given occupation. This is not a new phenomenon. It was noted as early as 1886 by the first commissioner of the U.S. Bureau of Labor Statistics.[1] At the turn of the century, Charles Booth called attention to the variations in the wages paid to workers within the same trades in London.[2] Large-scale wage surveys for use in the wage stabilization program during World War II revealed the pervasiveness of substantial occupational wage dispersion within local labor markets. The results of these surveys excited and perplexed many labor economists. Thus, Reynolds wrote that "it is always somewhat disturbing [in view of the assumed tendency toward wage equalization within labor markets] to observe the great variety of rates for apparently comparable jobs which prevails in actual labor markets."[3]

Private as well as government surveys reveal the existence of substantial occupational wage dispersion. With respect to surveys undertaken by employer associations, Tolles and Raimon remark that "any embarrassment of wage surveying associations is not because of the uniformity of the wages they report but, on the contrary, because their reports show, year after year, such a pervading diversity of wages."[4]

Actually, one would not expect to find uniformity of wage rates for particular jobs within labor markets even on the most rigid competitive assumptions. In a passage that tends to be overlooked, Marshall pointed out that "it is commonly said that the tendency of competition is to equalize the earnings of people engaged in the same trades or in trades of equal difficulty, but this statement requires to be interpreted carefully. For competition tends to make the earnings got by individuals of unequal efficiency in any given time, say, a day or a year, not equal, but unequal. . . ."[5] The point is that workers, even those with broadly the same training and skill, are not homogeneous in their ability or willingness to contribute to production, however production may be measured. This statement applies to workers in professional occupations as well as to those in relatively routine jobs.

It is quite difficult to obtain any precise measure of the range of individual differences in efficiency which is used here in a broad sense to embrace all of those attributes that contribute to a worker's performance on the job.[6] One approach is to observe in individual plants with sizable work forces the dispersion of earned rates of pay of employees compensated on a piece-rate basis on narrowly defined nonmachine-paced work. An example would be hand buttonhole-making in the men's coat and suit industry. An examination of the data for this operation in four establishments revealed a surprisingly wide dispersion of earned rates of pay (and hence of output) among individual workers within each establishment.[7] The coefficient of variation (as measured by the ratio of the standard deviation to the mean) ranged from 11 to 25 percent among the four establishments.

A broader investigation of output per hour in a variety of machine and hand operations in footwear and men's clothing manufacturing establishments, with the workers classified by age and sex, showed similar results.[8] With respect to age, this study showed that variations in the output of persons in the same age group were quite large; in fact, they were much greater than the differences in average output between the age groups.

There are various ways, within and among firms, by which some account can be taken of differences in efficiency among workers. The principal means are through wage systems providing variable rates of pay (incentive systems, rate ranges, personal rates) or, where single job rates are paid, by the careful selection of workers to meet established output standards.

Most workers (office and plant) are in establishments with formal wage or salary rate structures, which provide either a single rate or a range of rates for each job or labor grade within the establishment. In single rate structures, learners, apprentices, or probationary workers typically are paid below the applicable single rate and achieve the full job rate over a period of time. In rate range structures, inexperienced workers typically will enter at the bottom of the range; thereafter, their rates within the range will be determined by merit review, length of service, or a combination of these factors.

The most recent comprehensive data on the prevalence of various types of wage payment plans in American industry relate to the early 1960s.[9] At that time, about two-thirds of the office employees were in establishments with formal pay plans, almost all of which were rate-range plans. Among plant workers, 65 percent were employed in establishments with pay systems based on time rates; about 37 percent were covered by single rate plans and 28 percent by rate-range plans. Additionally, about 20 percent of the plant workers, mostly in manufacturing, were paid on an incentive basis. Some 35 percent of the office workers and 14 percent of the plant workers were in establishments without formal wage payment plans; that is, rates of pay were not established for jobs as such, but were attached to individual workers.

An analysis of wage payment provisions in 1,711 major collective bargaining agreements in effect January 1, 1976, begins with the statement that such provisions "have become increasingly complex. Workers may be compensated by fixed wage rates; automatic, merit, or combination automatic-merit progression arrangements; and piecework, mileage, and commission incentives . . . Many agreements provide special wage rates for handicapped and older workers, [and] personalized red-circle rates. . . . "[10] The study indicates that about 36 percent of the agreements contained provisions for rate ranges, and 27 percent for the use of incentive rather than time rates on at least some jobs. Additionally, about 6 percent of the agreements provided for compensation on a mileage or commission basis.[11]

In incentive pay systems, of course, pay tends to be related directly to output. Rate-range systems provide scope for variations in rates within jobs on the basis of individual efficiency. This is so even when movement from one step to the next within the range is based not on merit review but on length of service, which may serve as a rough measure of the increased value of a worker to the firm. In a most interesting analysis, Fogel argues that, in many situations, rate-range wage structures reflect the need not only to compensate for efficiency or quality differences among workers in the labor market, but also to satisfy their wage or salary expectations.[12] Even in establishments which, as a matter of policy, have single job rate structures, it is not unusual to discover wage rate differences within occupations. Such "personal" rates appear to reflect a powerful tendency for differential compensation to emerge.

In single job rate structures, however, the problem of employee selection is crucial. In machine-paced operations, for example, the workers selected must be capable of adapting themselves to the operating rates established by management or through collective bargaining. Typically in such situations, management has the authority within most collective bargaining agreements to select and, within a prescribed probationary period, to fire new employees. The retention of new employees thus can be made with reference to their ability to meet production standards for the jobs for which single rates are set.

The fact that workers of a given grade will differ in "quality"—that is, in their capacity or willingness to contribute to production—helps to explain differences in wage or salary levels among firms. Relatively high wage firms in a given industry and labor market will seek to recruit and retain superior workers. In their illuminating study of wage determination for female office employees in banking and insurance firms in Boston, Shultz and his associates pointed out that "the employers seemed uniformly convinced that, given a band of conceivable hiring rates where the top was about 110 percent of the bottom, the quality of girls you could hire for the top rate would clearly be superior."[13] With this as an operating assumption, employers pursued a variety of strategies with respect to the quality of the new employees they sought to hire.

It should be noted, however, that no sharp dichotomy in wage structure necessarily exists among establishments with distinctly different average wage levels. This is because the dispersion of rates of pay for particular jobs within establishments often results in substantial overlap of rates among establishments, even where the average levels differ. The extent to which intraestablishment wage differences contribute to total dispersion varies significantly among categories of occupations and labor markets. It appears to be substantially more important, for example, in the case of office than of plant jobs in manufacturing.[14]

In attempting to account for the dispersion of rates of pay within occupations, particular interest attaches to a study by Rees and Shultz which attempts, through regression analysis, to identify and measure factors contributing to wage dispersion in selected occupations in a local labor market.[15] The market consisted of Chicago and Gary-Hammond-East Chicago, with a labor force in 1960 of 2.8 million. A small random sample of establishments, stratified by size, was selected from a universe including manufacturing; transportation, communication and public utilities; wholesale and retail trade; finance, insurance, and real estate; and other service industries except private households. Three white-collar and nine manual occupations, all or most of which typically appear in cross-industry wage surveys, were chosen for study. Supplementary nonrandom samples were drawn for two of these occupations with relatively heavy employment in specialized firms.

The wage data, expressed as earnings per hour worked in 1963, were obtained by personal visit. The distinctive feature of the survey was the collection of a large quantity of information on the characteristics of individual workers, including age, sex, race, marital status, education, seniority with firm, experience or training, and place of residence.

On the whole, the findings of the study were unexceptionable. For most occupations, wages were positively associated with seniority, previous experience on the present job, education, and age up to some maximum age. In general, seniority was the single most powerful variable. Wages were lower for women than for men and, in general, for nonwhites and workers with Spanish surnames than for whites in those occupations for which these comparisons could be made.

For some of the selected occupations, the addition of establishment variables—location, industry, unionization, and size—added substantially to the explanatory power of the regression equations. The equations including both individual and establishment variables "explained" from about 43 percent (maintenance electricians) to 66 percent (material handlers) of the variance in wages per hour at work in the survey occupations, except for truck drivers where the proportion, for several plausible reasons, was markedly lower.

From their study of factors influencing occupational wage dispersion, and of more general aspects of labor market behavior in Chicago, Rees and Shultz conclude that "the actors in the market—the workers, the employers, the unions, and the job market intermediaries—behave on the whole in rational ways."[16] The major weakness of the study is the small size of the sample in relation to the universe, especially for the use of variables reflecting establishment characteristics. Nevertheless, it provides some sense of the quantitative importance of a variety of factors affecting wage dispersion in different types of jobs and a corrective to excessively "institutional" views of the labor market.

It must be said emphatically that not all of the dispersion in rates of pay for particualr occupations within a given labor market can be attributed to differences in worker efficiency or quality. However, such differences do appear to be taken importantly into account in methods of wage payment and in personnel selection and administration. But in addition, dispersion also reflects labor market imperfections, compensating advantages or disadvantages of employment among firms or industries, and trade union influence on the wage levels and internal wage structures of particular firms. It should be pointed out also that even within closely defined occupations (e.g., order clerk) duties may vary somewhat from one firm to another, depending on size of firm, product, and other factors, and these variations may affect pay. A statistical survey of wages by occupation must classify workers on the basis of their principal activities and cannot, either within or among firms, account for marginal differences in duties and responsibilities. Hence, one source of dispersion is inherent in the statistics.

Suggested Readings

Wage rate dispersion within occupations is complex and has not been extensively studied. An article by Eaton H. Conant, "Worker

Efficiency and Wage Differentials in a Clerical Labor Market," *Industrial and Labor Relations Review,* April 1963, provides a useful supplement to the text references. James E. Buckley, in "Intra-occupational Wage Dispersion in Metropolitan Areas, 1967–68," *Monthly Labor Review,* September 1969, suggests several reasons for variation in dispersion rates among labor markets.

Recent data on the proportion of factory workers under various types of wage payment systems are contained in U.S. Bureau of Labor Statistics, Report 516, *Wage Payment Plans in Manufacturing Industries* (Washington, D.C., 1977).

7

The Trend of Money and Real Wages, 1800–1978

Over the course of more than a century and a half, the American system has yielded higher levels of both money and real wages to the working population. The rise has not been uninterrupted. The present chapter seeks broadly to trace the movement of money and real wages from 1800 to the present. Since changes in real wages are profoundly influenced by changes in labor productivity, a brief review of our productivity experience follows these introductory remarks.

The measurement of changes in the level of money and real wages over an extended period has many ambiguities. This would be true even if the statistics of money wages, consumer prices, and productivity were much more adequate than, for most periods, they in fact are. The basic reasons for these ambiguities lie in the enormous changes that have occurred during the period under review in the composition of the national output of goods and services, in patterns of consumption, in the growth and deployment of the labor force among occupations and industries, and in the shift from a largely rural to a predominantly urban society.

The date in this chapter on the course of money and real wages from 1800 to 1978 are presented for a number of subperiods. The selection of these subperiods was dictated to a considerable extent by the quantity and reliability of the data available, but they also broadly reflect phases in our economic development. No continuous general index of money wages can be constructed with any confidence for the period as a whole. An annual index of consumer prices is available for the period since 1800, formed by splicing a number of privately compiled indexes to the official Consumer Price Index, which dates only from 1913.[1] Use is made of this index for various periods, with reference at several places to other price indexes put together by private investigators. The subperiods for which data are presented in this chapter on the movement of money wages, consumer prices, and real wages are 1800–1860, 1860–1900, 1900–1947, and 1947–1978.

The general level of money wages for the economy as a whole, or for an important sector, such as manufacturing, is as great an abstraction as the concept of the general price level for, say, consumer goods. It represents, in principle, a weighted average of the numerous rates of pay that attach to individuals and occupations in the economy or the sector. It is, however, a most useful abstraction, for over periods of time, in the form of an appropriate index, it provides a measure of the changing level of money wages. Such an index, when adjusted for changes in the level of consumer prices, provides insight into changes in real wages and hence in living standards. It fails to provide a full measure of change in living standards, for it does not take into account any reduction in hours of work (i.e., increase in leisure) that has occurred. Nor does it account for the fact that, during the period since World War II, employer expenditures on supplementary benefits, as shown in Chapter 2, increased more rapidly than on direct wages.

Real Wages and Productivity

Real wages in the United States have increased over most of our national history. The key to this advance has been the long-term rise in productivity in American industry and agriculture.[2] Productivity reflects the influence of a host of factors, including physical capital formation; technical progress, with its roots in basic and applied research; education and training of the work force (in modern terms, investment in human capital); worker motivation and morale; economies of scale in production from wider markets and the greater specialization of workers, plant, and equipment; and governmental policies bearing on incentives (or disincentives) for investment and innovation.

At the beginning of its national existence, underlying economic conditions in the United States provided powerful encouragement to growth in productivity. The essential condition was the shortage of labor relative to other factors of production. This clearly was sensed by Adam Smith, who observed in *The Wealth of Nations* that "the wages of labor . . . are much higher in North America than in any part of England."[3] He cited as typical the daily earnings in colonial currency and in sterling of common laborers and of craftsmen such as ship carpenters, house carpenters, bricklayers, and tailors in the province of New York. Not only were money wages higher in the colonies, but "the prices of provisions is everywhere in North America much lower than in England."[4] Consequently, "the real command of the necessities and conveniences of life" was even greater than the difference in money wages would suggest. Smith attributed this situation to the abundance of land and the relative scarcity of labor.[5]

Much general evidence—the development of internal transportation, the growth of markets, specific inventions and their diffusion, the rise of various manufacturing industries, the changing composition of the labor force—points unmistakably to productivity growth during the first part of the nineteenth century. Some quantitative estimates of productivity advance between 1800 and the beginning of the Civil War are also available. Thus, David estimates that the average annual rate of growth of real output per capita exceeded 1.0 percent but probably was less than 1.5 percent between 1800 and 1840, and about 1.5 percent for 1840–60.[6] Gallman estimates that the output of commodities per worker (agriculture, mining, manufacturing, and construction) increased about 35 percent between 1839 and 1859, with about two-thirds of the gain occurring during the 1850s.[7]

Writing in 1865, a keen English observer related American invention to high wages and labor shortages. In the words of Sir S. Morton Peto:

> The high rate of wages, and indeed I may say the absolute absence, in many cases, of work people to take wages, has stimulated invention. Mechanical contrivances of every sort are produced to supply the want of human hands. Thus we find America producing a machine even to peel apples; another to beat eggs; a third to clean knives; a fourth to wring clothes; in fact, human hands have scarcely been engaged in any

67

employment in which some cheap and efficient labour-saving machine does not now, to some extent, replace them.[8]

Productivity advance continued after the Civil War to the end of the century, with the completion of transcontinental rail links, marked growth in agricultural output, and manufacturing gains underpinned by great advances in technology. Decennial estimates by Dewhurst and his associates of output per man-hour for the private economy show an increase of about 79 percent from 1860 to 1900, with most of the increase occurring during the second half of the period.[9] This would indicate an average annual rate of growth of about 1.5 percent. Gallman estimates that commodity output per worker in agriculture, mining, manufacturing, and construction increased about 82 percent between 1859 and 1899.[10] This estimate approximates the broader estimate of Dewhurst and associates, which included segments of the economy in which productivity might be expected to lag behind that experienced by the goods-producing industries.

Again taking a long view, the rate of productivity increase from the beginning of the twentieth century through World War II appears to have exceeded the nineteenth-century rate. It is estimated that output per man-hour in the private economy grew by 172 percent between 1900 and 1947.[11] This would represent an average annual rate of increase of about 2.2 percent. During this period, the most rapid increase, at an average annual rate of 2.4 percent, occurred during the depression decade of the 1930s, but the average annual increase of 2.1 percent between 1910 and 1930 was also impressive.

National productivity experience following World War II deserves somewhat greater attention within the framework of this monograph. Table 7.1 shows the index of output per hour from 1947 to 1978 of all persons in the private business sector[12] of the economy, as prepared by the Bureau of Labor Statistics. It also shows year-to-year percentage changes in output per hour, and average annual rates of change for specified periods. It should be noted that by 1947 conversion from war to peacetime production had been largely completed.

Over the whole period from 1947 to 1978 output per hour more than doubled. The average annual rate of change was 2.7 percent. This was significantly higher than the rates derived from national productivity estimates relating either to the nineteenth century or to the twentieth century through World War II.

Table 7.1. **Index of Output per Hour and Year-to-Year Percentage Changes,
Private Business Sector, 1947–78** (1967=100)

Year	Index	Year-to-year percentage change	Year	Index	Year-to-year percentage change
1947	52.3		1963	87.7	3.9
1948	54.4	4.0	1964	91.3	4.1
1949	55.3	1.7	1965	94.7	3.7
1950	59.7	8.0	1966	97.8	3.3
1951	61.5	3.0	1967	100.0	2.2
1952	63.0	2.4	1968	103.3	3.3
1953	65.3	3.7	1969	103.7	0.4
1954	66.5	1.8	1970	104.5	0.8
1955	69.2	4.1	1971	107.8	3.2
1956	70.2	1.4	1972	111.0	3.0
1957	72.3	3.0	1973	113.1	1.9
1958	74.2	2.6	1974	109.9	-2.9
1959	76.8	3.5	1975	111.8	1.7
1960	78.1	1.7	1976	116.5	4.2
1961	80.6	3.2	1977	118.2	1.5
1962	84.4	4.7	1978	119.2	0.8

Average annual rates of increase:

1947–78	2.7%
1947–66	3.3
1966–78	1.7

Source: U.S. Department of Labor, Bureau of Labor Statistics.

As Table 7.1 shows, there was a marked difference in the rate of productivity increase between 1947–66 and 1966–78. During the first period, the rate of increase was 3.3 percent, as compared with 1.7 percent during the second period, a reduction of about one-half in the average annual rate of growth.

The causes for this slowdown are complex and to some extent conjectural. One cause was a sharp decline in the shift of manpower from agriculture to nonfarm industries, where, for the most part, output per hour is higher. Another cause may be the dilution of the labor force with many untrained entrants from the "baby boom" of the immediate postwar years and from the ranks of older women. Moreover, the 1960s may have witnessed shifts in attitudes among some segments of the labor force toward jobs and work that were not conducive to high standards of performance. It seems likely that the persistent inflation beginning in the mid-1960s contributed to the decline in the rate of productivity growth, for inflation adds to the uncertainties inherent in business planning and can inhibit capital formation and equity investment. It contributes also to social unrest, which has repercussions in the labor market and on attitudes toward work. Governmental regulations in a number of areas, including environment and work safety, which have costs as well as benefits, appear to have been a cause of the slowdown. Finally, the high productivity performance of the first part of the postwar period may have reflected the flowering of technological innovations that had their roots in the dismal 1930s and the war years.

Two general points are worth making with respect to the historical record on productivity change. First, the rate of change tends to fluctuate substantially from year to year and over longer periods. The second column of Table 7.1 shows that the rate of productivity change during the period 1947–78 ranged from a decline of almost 3 percent between 1973 and 1974 to an increase of 8 percent between 1949 and 1950. Over short periods, productivity is greatly influenced by the business cycle, tending to rise at less than the average rate during periods of contraction and at above the average rate during the expansion phase of the cycle. Hence figures for a single year are of limited significance.

But there are also longer swings in the rate of productivity growth that may well extend over more than one cycle in business activity. We have already noticed that the average growth rate for 1947–66, which included four recessions, was distinctly higher than for the years 1966–78, which was marked by two recessions. During the nineteenth century, the average increase in productivity appears to have been particularly impressive during the periods 1820–40, 1850–60, and 1880–1900, and, in the first half of the twentieth century, between 1910 and 1940.

Second, although productivity experience underlies gains in real wages, most money wage decisions are not in fact related in any explicit way to the secular rate of national productivity growth. What this rate tells us is the extent to which the consumption of goods and services and leisure, or some combination of these, can be increased in the economy as a whole. How productivity gains are actually distributed as between labor and property income, or among different groups of workers within the labor force, is a function of money wage and price determination. As shown in Chapter 8, however, the national productivity rate in the post-World War II period has assumed explicit importance in a certain type of wage settlement, and underlies efforts by the federal government to formulate national "incomes" policies.

Wage Trends—the Nineteenth Century

Continuous data on rates of pay are extremely limited for the 60 years preceding the Civil War. The most extensive collection has been provided by Lebergott in the form of money wage series, admittedly rough, for a number of employee groups for all or part of the period.[13]

In summary, Lebergott's data suggest a marked decline in money wages by 1819 as compared with 1800. These years included the great disturbances to trade occasioned by the Embargo Act of 1807 and the War of 1812. The closing years of the period were marked by a severe economic crisis, and it is probable that much of the decline in money wages occurred during that period.[14] Between 1819 and 1832, money wages appear to have regained the levels of 1800. A further rise took place to 1850 and between 1850 and 1860.

For the period 1840–60, the wage series assembled by the Bureau of Labor Statistics for the celebrated Aldrich Report[15] confirm Lebergott's general impression of a rise in money wages. These data are exceedingly thin, however, for the investigation was made in the early 1890s and involved the collection of occupational wage rates from a few establishments with long-term payroll records. However, the Bureau secured continuous annual data from 1840 from one or more establishments in the building trades, carriages and wagons, cotton goods, illuminating gas, lumber, metals and metallic goods, railroads, stone, and white lead. An index weighted by industry employment reveals, with few interruptions, an upward drift of money wages over the 1840–60 period aggregating about 20 percent.[16] This upward movement generally is confirmed by additional wage data collected by Joseph D. Weeks for the Aldrich Report from a few establishments in the coal, iron, glass, and pottery industries,[17] and by information for several communities on school teacher salaries.[18]

While money wages appear to have risen moderately between 1800 and 1860, taking the period as a whole, the cost of living undoubtedly dropped sharply. As in the case of wages, the price data are somewhat tenuous. But two differently constructed indexes of consumer prices, one prepared by Lebergott[19] and the other by Hoover,[20] both show declines in the neighborhood of 50 percent between 1800 and 1860.

In view of the fragile nature of both the wage and price series for the 1800–60 period, a precise estimate fo the change in real wages would be hazardous. It seems reasonably clear, however, that the purchasing power of money wages increased substantially over the period as a whole. Lebergott presents the following "highly speculative" estimate of change:[21]

Period	Percentage change in real wages
1800-20	0
1820-32	25
1832-50	25
1850-60	1

Spread over the entire period, the above estimates represent an average annual increase in real wages of about 0.8 percent. This estimate does not appear inconsistent with the productivity estimates for the period, as discussed in the preceding section of this chapter. It reflects, again taking the period as a whole, a moderate rise in money wages, but primarily a falling price level for consumer goods.

During the six decades beginning with 1800, the population of the United States increased from about 5.3 million to 31.5 million persons. The total labor force 10 years of age and older, as estimated by Lebergott, rose from 1.9 million in 1800 to 11.1 million.in 1860, with slaves in the latter year constituting about 21 percent of the total.[22] In 1800, only about 10 percent of the gainfully employed worked for wages, the remainder consisting of farmers, self-employed mechanics, small tradesmen, and slaves. By 1860, the proportion of wage earners had risen to more than 30 percent, reflecting the development of transportation, the rise of industry, and the growth of urbanization. Employment in manufacturing, which was almost negligible in 1800, reached about 1.3 million in 1860.

The Period 1860–1900

Both money and real wages, with some interruptions, continued to advance during the remainder of the nineteenth century. There is considerable uncertainty as to the magnitude of the advance, for the volume and quality of the underlying data, although somewhat better than for the 1800–1860 period, are far from satisfactory. The Aldrich Report is the major source of data on the trend of wages for the years

1860–90. These data, as most recently reworked by Long, are shown in Table 7.2 in the form of index numbers of average daily wages in manufacturing.[23] For the final decade of the period, an index of average daily earnings in manufacturing, constructed by Rees, has been spliced to this series.[24] The Long series has been subjected to formidable criticism by Lebergott,[25] who has prepared a series of average annual earnings for "nonfarm employees" from 1860 to 1900.[26] This series also is shown in Table 7.2, together with the consumer price index compiled by Hoover for 1860–90 to which is linked an index constructed by Rees for the remaining years to 1900.[27]

Table 7.2 indicates thàt prices outpaced wages during the Civil War and real wages therefore fell. The level of prices peaked in 1864, and in that year average real wages in manufacturing, as measured by the Long-Rees series, were almost 30 percent below their 1860 level. The decline in the Lebergott nonfarm series was less sharp, about 20 percent. The prewar level of real wages, as measured by Long-Rees, was regained in manufacturing by 1868, a position not achieved in the broader nonfarm series of Lebergott until 1871.

The two money wage series behave rather differently for the years 1864–73, but each shows a decline of about 17 percent between 1873 and 1880, years of generally depressed business conditions and relatively high unemployment. By 1880, consumer prices had fallen almost 40 percent from their Civil War peak and were only about 7 percent above the 1860 level.

From 1880 until the end of the century, money wages in manufacturing increased substantially, with some interruption during the comparatively mild recession that accompanied the crisis of 1883 and during the severe depression of the 1890s. The annual earnings series for nonfarm employees rose slowly during the 1880s, but fell rather sharply between 1892 and 1894. Consumer prices in 1900 were 13 percent below their 1880 level. The wage and earnings series show sizable increases in real terms between 1880 and 1900, for manufacturing by 37 percent and for nonfarm employees by 44 percent.

For the 1860–1900 period as a whole, years of considerable economic turbulence, average daily wages in manufacturing, as measured by the Long-Rees series, increased by 54 percent; consumer prices declined by 7 percent; and the advance in real wages was 66 percent. The average annual rates of change were 1.5 percent in money wages, −0.2 percent in consumer prices, and 1.7 percent in real

Table 7.2. Indexes of Average Daily Wages in Manufacturing, Average Annual Earnings for Nonfarm Employees, and Consumer Prices, 1860–1900

(1860=100)

Year	Average daily wages, manufacturing		Average annual earnings, nonfarm employees		Consumer prices
	Money	Real	Money	Real	
1860	100	100	100	100	100
1861	99	99	102	102	100
1862	104	94	106	96	111
1863	110	80	126	92	137
1864	124	71	139	80	174
1865	138	81	141	83	170
1866	145	89	135	83	163
1867	147	94	132	85	156
1868	149	101	137	93	148
1869	151	102	137	93	148
1870	151	107	135	96	141
1871	153	115	133	100	133
1872	154	116	134	101	133
1873	156	117	128	96	133
1874	151	120	121	96	126
1875	145	119	117	96	122
1876	141	118	111	93	119
1877	134	113	107	90	119
1878	128	120	104	97	107
1879	125	120	103	99	104
1880	130	121	106	99	107
1881	131	122	113	106	107
1882	134	125	118	110	107
1883	138	133	121	116	104
1884	140	140	121	121	100

Table 7.2. (continued)

Year	Average daily wages, manufacturing		Average annual earnings, nonfarm employees		Consumer prices
	Money	Real	Money	Real	
1885	136	136	123	123	100
1886	136	136	125	125	100
1887	141	141	127	127	100
1888	142	142	128	128	100
1889	146	146	130	130	100
1890	148	148	131	131	100
1891	150	150	132	132	100
1892	150	150	133	133	100
1893	156	156	126	126	100
1894	142	148	116	121	96
1895	142	153	121	130	93
1896	146	157	121	130	93
1897	143	154	122	131	93
1898	140	151	121	130	93
1899	149	160	129	139	93
1900	154	166	133	143	93
Average annual rates of change:					
1860–1900	1.5	1.7	0.7	0.9	-0.2

Source: For wages: Clarence D. Long, *Wages and Earnings in the United States, 1860–90* (Princeton, N.J.: Princeton University Press, 1960), table A-1, pp. 121–24; Albert Rees, *Real Wages in Manufacturing, 1890–1914* (Princeton, N.J.: Princeton University Press, 1961), table 10, p. 33; Stanley Lebergott, *Manpower in Economic Growth* (New York: McGraw-Hill, 1964), table A-19, p. 528. For consumer prices: U.S. Department of Labor, Bureau of Labor Statistics, Bulletin 1865, *Handbook of Labor Statistics 1975* (Washington, D.C.: GPO, 1975), table 122, p. 313.

wages. The Lebergott series of average annual earnings for nonfarm employees show increases of 33 percent in money and 43 percent in real terms over the 1860–1900 period, or annual rates of about 0.7 and 0.9, respectively.

These figures should not be interpreted with much precision, but they do indicate that a substantial advance in both money and real wages occurred during the years from 1860 to 1900. Productivity in the economy appears to have increased sufficiently, taking the period as a whole, to provide for significant improvement in real rates of pay and living standards. Gallman's estimates of commodity output per worker, cited in the preceding section, lend some support to the showing of the Long-Rees daily wage series in manufacturing, in contrast with the Lebergott nonfarm series, that the decline in real wages during the Civil War had been overcome by the end of the 1860s, and that advances were made during the following decade. Long points to a great increase in capital per worker during the 1880s as helping to explain the sharp rise in productivity and real wages during that decade,[28] when annual earnings as measured by Lebergott also increased markedly.

The supply side of the labor market expanded rapidly during this period, with the total labor force in 1900 more than two and a half times its size in 1860. Immigration contributed heavily to labor force increase, and Lebergott places considerable (short-run) emphasis on immigration as a retarding factor in real wage advance. Long points more generally to the large increase in labor supply during this period. The abolition of slavery represented a great social change in labor market institutions, affecting directly, at the beginning of the period, about one-fifth of the labor force. There were also, of course, important changes in the occupational and industrial composition of the working population. In manufacturing, employment increased almost four times between 1860 and 1900.[29]

Some Aspects of the Nineteenth Century Experience

There are several aspects of the nineteenth century experience that are worth emphasis.

1. The labor market was highly competitive, except for the institution of slavery, which was swept away by the Civil War. The market

expanded and became more complex as the century progressed. Governmental influence on the market in the form of social legislation or other types of intervention was minimal. Trade union power was weak and sporadic, with a remarkable but short-lived labor upsurge occurring under the Knights of Labor during the 1880s. The foundations of modern trade unionism under the American Federation of Labor also were laid in that decade. But total trade union membership by 1897 was less than half a million.[30] There undoubtedly was, as Ozanne has argued in a remarkable study,[31] union impact on wages in particular situations and at particular times during the post-Civil War period, but for the most part the labor bargin was struck between individual workers and their employers. To the extent that bargaining power as commonly understood as a factor, its preponderance generally must have rested with the employers.

2. Nevertheless, as we have seen, real wages advanced significantly during the nineteenth century. Although the available statistics on money wages and prices are such that any estimate must be tentative, real wages appear to have at least doubled between 1800 and 1900. The advance was uneven. There were periods during which the level of real wages either failed to increase or actually declined, but the century as a whole witnessed substantial gains in living standards among the working population.

3. The behavior of money wages and consumer prices which produced this result was divergent. Despite a large increase in labor supply, to which immigration contributed heavily at certain periods, and the absence of effective trade union organization, money rates of pay rose over the century as a whole. There were periods of decline, notably during the first two decades of the century and during the 1870s and 1890s, but the trend during the 100-year period was upward. Consumer prices behaved differently. As nearly as one can judge, their level fell between 1800 and 1860, rose sharply during the Civil War, and then declined to the end of the century. During the decade 1890–99 the level of consumer prices was in the neighborhood of 40 percent lower than the level during 1800–1809. Conceding all of the weaknesses and ambiguities in price measurement over the period, the direction and general magnitude of the movement seems unassailable.[32]

The advance in real wages over the century, therefore, reflected the interaction of a long-term rise in money wages and a fall in the level of consumer prices. Over this period, many new products came on the market and old products were improved or fell into disuse, thus complicating any interpretation of changes in living standards.[33]

4. Underlying the rise in real wages was growth in the productivity of the American economy. This growth was rooted in a variety of factors, including an abundance of land and other natural resources; a relative scarcity of labor, which stimulated technological innovations and their application to both agriculture and industry; the generation of capital from internal saving and investment but also from the inflow of funds from abroad; an incessant drive for "internal improvements" in the form of roads, canals, and railroads, which broadened markets and facilitated economies of scale; governmental policies designed to encourage economic growth, including the creation of the corporate form of enterprise; and the energy and resourcefulness of the working population.

5. The labor market during the nineteenth century, although highly competitive, had certain characteristics that tended to make for higher real rates of pay. There was, first, an extraordinary mobility of labor, which was related to the existence of a range of alternative job opportunities and particularly to the availability of free or cheap land in the West. Even the large influx during the second half of the century of mainly unskilled immigrant workers, in part recruited directly by employers, only partially reduced the relative scarcity of labor. The greater development of technology during the nineteenth century in American as compared with British industry, as Habakkuk has shown, owes much to this labor market condition.[34]

There was, second, an absence of strong conventional or traditional standards of pay for particular jobs or skills that marked wage structures in the older economies of Europe. This was related to the absence of social hierarchies in the United States, which in the labor market "created incessant pressure toward higher wages. For there was no 'proper' social position for an American, so there could be no 'proper' wage for him,"[35] The importance of this factor cannot be measured in quantitative terms, but the absence of deep-rooted social demarcations must have had an impact on worker behavior in the labor market.

Wage Trends—the Twentieth Century

The Period 1900–1947

The end of the nineteenth century saw the end of our geographical frontier, and the contrast between the iron furnaces and forges of the early 1800s and the formation of the United States Steel Corporation in 1901 reflected the magnitude of our industrial revolution. The twentieth century, which was welcomed with great fanfare, ushered in another era of extraordinary economic and social change.

Between 1900 and 1947, with which this section is concerned, two world wars occurred, together with a depression, during the 1930s, of unprecedented severity. A highly restrictive immigration policy was adopted after World War I. As in the nineteenth century, technological progress was marked. The Panama Canal, an engineering feat of immense difficulty, was completed in 1914. Whole new industries arose. The automobile, especially with the advent of Ford's Model T, began to reshape the configuration of urban areas and of labor markets. By 1947, air transport was beginning to challenge railroad passenger service. The radio had introduced an entirely new dimension into entertainment and communication.

As a labor market institution, trade unionism remained relatively weak until the latter part of the 1930s. Wolman estimates that organization among nonfarm employees reached 9.9 percent by 1910, climbed to 19.4 percent in the upsurge that accompanied World War I, and thereafter declined to 10.2 percent by 1930.[36] Organization was heavily concentrated, even in 1920, in building, transportation, mining, clothing, and printing.[37]

The depression of the 1930s brought with it a resurgence of union organization, stimulated in part by the famous Section 7(a) of the National Industrial Recovery Act (NIRA) of 1933, which asserted the right of workers, under codes of fair competition, to organize and bargain collectively. The NIRA was declared unconstitutional in May 1935, but the National Labor Relations Act was passed two months later. When the constitutionality of that act was established in 1937, powerful legal sanction was given to the right of self-organization and of the duty of employers to bargain in good faith over wages and other terms of employment. Union membership expanded after 1935 and

79

especially during the full employment years of World War II. By 1947, the Bureau of Labor Statistics estimated the total membership of American unions (exclusive of Canadian membership) at 14.8 million, representing about 34 percent of employment in nonfarm establishments.

Social legislation, much of which had labor market implications, advanced rapidly at the state level during the early decades of the twentieth century, especially with respect to the employment and hours of work of women and children. In 1912, Massachusetts enacted the first minimum wage law in the United States. This initiative was followed by a number of other states, but was arrested when such legislation was declared unconstitutional by the Supreme Court in 1923. Social insurance, again at the state level, was inaugurated in 1910 by New York legislation for the compensation of workers for industrial injuries in a limited number of occupations. Workmen's compensation laws spread with relative rapidity.

The traumatic experience of the great depression of the 1930s revolutionized the role of the federal government in labor and social legislation. The United States Employment Service was established as a federal-state enterprise in 1933 for the purpose of providing a unified system of employment exchanges. The passage of the National Labor Relations Act in 1935 has already been mentioned. Also in 1935 the Congress passed the Social Security Act, with provision for a federal-state unemployment insurance system and for a federal system of old-age pensions. In 1938, the Fair Labor Standards Act was passed to provide minimum wages and a basic 40-hour week, with premium pay for excess hours, for covered employees in private industry. It was preceded by two pieces of legislation for government determination of wage standards for employees of specific classes of federal contractors.

Such, very briefly, were some of the main forces bearing on the wage position of American workers between 1900 and the end of World War II. Unfortunately, the wage statistics available for this period, taken as a whole, remain, as in the nineteenth century, somewhat less than satisfactory for a precise charting of wage behavior for the working population. They include periodic studies by the Bureau of Labor Statistics of rates or earnings in selected industries, and, beginning in 1915, a slowly expanding program of monthly reports on employment and payrolls by industry; the pioneering study by Douglas of the movement of money and real wages from 1890 to 1926 for major segments of employment;[38] and the study by Rees, previously cited, of real wages in manufacturing from 1890 to 1914.

An impression of the course of wages from 1900 to 1947 is provided by the selected wage index series shown in Table 7.3. The first of these is of average hourly earnings for production and related workers in manufacturing, obtained by splicing the series compiled by Rees for the years 1900–1914 to the Bureau of Labor Statistics series for the subsequent years to 1947. The Douglas average hourly earnings series for "all industry" for 1900–1926 is also shown, and an average annual salaries series for public school teachers prepared by Douglas to 1926 and by the Bureau of Labor Statistics for later years. The index of union scales in the building trades was compiled by the Bureau of Labor Statistics. It should be noted that only this latter index, with some qualifications, approximates a wage rate series; the others are earnings series, and are affected by such factors as changes in industry and occupational composition (especially in manufacturing), overtime and other forms of premium pay, and shifts in industry location. The Consumer Price Index from 1900 to 1912 is that constructed by Rees and for subsequent years by the Bureau of Labor Statistics.

It will be observed from Table 7.3 that there was a substantial upward movement in both money and real wages between 1900 and the outbreak in 1914 of World War I. In manufacturing, average hourly earnings rose by about 45 percent—in money terms, the rise was from 15.1 cents to 22.0 cents—over this 14-year period; the increase in real earnings was about 21 percent, or at an average annual rate of 1.3 percent. The "all-industry" index of average hourly earnings from Douglas in general confirms this comparatively rapid advance. Public school teachers did exceptionally well during this period; their index of real average annual salaries, helped by an increase in the average length of the school year, rose about 43 percent. The data on union wage scales in the building trades begin with 1907; between that year and 1914, average scales, in real terms, increased by 18 percent.

Then came World War I, which had a marked impact on the American economy long before our actual involvement in 1917. Unfortunately, there is a four-year hiatus, 1915–18, in the manu-

Table 7.3. Indexes of Average Hourly Earnings, Factory Workers and All Industry, Union Wage Scales, Building Trades, Average Annual Salaries, Public School Teachers, and Consumer Prices, 1900–1947 (1914=100)

Year	Average hourly earnings, factory workers		Average hourly earnings, all industry		Union wage scales, building trades		Average annual salaries, public school teachers		Consumer prices
	Money	Real	Money	Real	Money	Real	Money	Real	
1900	69	83	72	87			58	70	83
1901	72	87	74	89			60	72	83
1902	75	87	77	90			61	71	86
1903	77	86	81	90			63	70	90
1904	77	86	81	90			67	74	90
1905	78	87	83	92			70	78	90
1906	84	93	86	96			73	81	90
1907	87	94	89	96	79	85	76	82	93
1908	84	93	88	98	84	93	81	90	90
1909	85	94	89	99	88	98	84	93	90
1910	90	97	91	98	92	99	87	94	93
1911	92	99	93	100	92	99	90	97	93
1912	94	98	96	100	93	100	94	98	96
1913	101	102	99	100	95	99	97	98	99
1914	100	100	100	100	97	98	100	100	100
1915			101	100	100	100	102	101	101
1916			110	101	101	100	107	98	109
1917			125	98	104	95	115	90	128
1918			153	102	110	86	122	81	150
1919	214	124	177	103	122	81	144	84	172
1920	243	125	218	110	141	82	166	83	199
1921	230	129	203	114	189	95	192	108	178
1922	218	131	192	115	193	108	211	126	167
1923	234	138	209	123	181	108	217	128	170
1924	245	144	216	127	200	118	221	130	170
1925	245	141	220	126	215	127	224	129	174
					224	128			

Table 7.3. (continued)

Year	Average hourly earnings, factory workers		Average hourly earnings, all industry		Union wage scales, building trades		Average annual salaries, public school teachers		Consumer prices
	Money	Real	Money	Real	Money	Real	Money	Real	
1926	245	139	225	128	239	136	226	128	176
1927	246	142			247	143	233	135	173
1928	252	148			248	146			170
1929	253	149			251	148	242	142	170
1930	247	149			262	158			166
1931	230	151			262	172	251	165	152
1932	200	147			225	165			136
1933	198	154			218	169	233	181	129
1934	238	179			220	165			133
1935	246	179			222	162	224	164	137
1936	249	180			230	167			138
1937	279	195			246	172	233	163	143
1938	281	201			268	191			140
1939	284	209			270	199	250	184	136
1940	296	211			275	196			140
1941	329	224			285	194	259	176	147
1942	385	238			302	186			162
1943	433	252			304	177	268	156	172
1944	457	261			307	175			175
1945	460	257			313	175	294	164	179
1946	486	251			349	180			194
1947	551	248			399	180	337	152	222

Sources: Manufacturing wages, 1900–14, Albert Rees, *Real Wages in Manufacturing, 1890–1914* (Princeton, N.J.: Princeton University Press, 1961), table 10, p. 33; 1914–47, Bureau of Labor Statistics. All industry wages, 1900–26, Paul H. Douglas, *Real Wages in the United States, 1890–1926* (Boston: Houghton, Mifflin Co., 1930), table 73, p. 205. Building trades union scales, 1907–47, Bureau of Labor Statistics. Public school teacher salaries, 1900–26, Douglas, *op. cit.*, table 142, p. 382; 1926–47, Bureau of Labor Statistics. Consumer prices, Bureau of Labor Statistics.

facturing wage series shown in Table 7.3. By 1920, at the height of the postwar boom, the level of hourly earnings for factory workers was two and a half times higher than in 1914. The broader Douglas series shows a lesser movement, increasing by 118 percent. Union scales in building increased by 89 percent and the average annual salaries of teachers by only 66 percent. Consumer prices almost exactly doubled between 1914 and 1920.

Judging by the Douglas "all-industry" series, the working population as a whole about held its own in terms of real wages during the war period, but registered gains during the immediate postwar boom. But some groups fell behind. Public school teachers and building trades workers experienced substantial losses in purchasing power between 1914 and 1920, but the real wage position of both groups improved markedly between 1920 and 1921.

The post-World War I boom collapsed toward the end of 1920, and a short-lived recession ensued. Among the series shown in Table 7.3, money wages fell between 1920 and 1922, except for public school teachers. The decline was 12 percent for both the manufacturing and the Douglas "all-industry" series, and about 4 percent for union scales in building. Consumer prices, however, declined about 16 percent, so that real hourly wages or earnings appear to have increased generally during these years. Additional gains in real wages, notably in the case of the building trades, were registered during the remainder of the 1920s.

Between 1929 and 1947, the economy was dominated, first, by the most severe depression in United States history, and then, second, by World War II and, in its immediate aftermath, by reconversion from war to peacetime production. Unemployment in 1929 was estimated at 3.2 percent of the civilian labor force; by 1933, the rate reached the staggering figure of almost 25 percent and remained above 14 percent for the remainder of the decade. It began falling sharply with the inauguration of our defense program in mid-1940 and dropped below 2 percent during 1943–45. In 1947, the unemployment rate was 3.6 percent.[39]

In view of the high unemployment rate throughout the 1930s, one might have expected an almost constant decline in money wages. In manufacturing, as Table 7.3 shows, average hourly earnings did drop about 22 percent between 1929 and 1933. But they recovered sharply between 1933 and 1936, reflecting some improvement in the job situation and New Deal recovery measures. Another marked rise occurred between 1936 and 1937, stimulated at least in part by an upsurge in trade union organization and militancy. In 1939, the hourly earnings of factory workers were about 12 percent above the 1929 level.

In building, union wage scales actually advanced between 1929 and 1931, fell over the next two years, and then rebounded by 1939 to about 8 percent above the 1929 level. By 1939, the average salaries of public school teachers, after a decline between 1931 and 1935, were 3 percent above the 1929 level.

In the meantime, the level of consumer prices declined by 24 percent between 1929 and 1933. There was a modest recovery thereafter, but in 1939 consumer prices remained 20 percent below their level of a decade earlier. As a result of these divergent movements of money wages and retail prices, real wages, for those with employment, were markedly higher in 1939 than in 1929. The rise in terms of hourly earnings for factory workers was 40 percent; of union scales in building, 34 percent; and of annual salaries for public school teachers, 30 percent.

When World War II began in September 1939, the United States had large unemployed resources of manpower and of plant and equipment. Our actual involvement in the conflict, and hence the extent of our military and economic commitment, was not irrevocably determined until December 7, 1941, when the Japanese attacked Pearl Harbor. But as previously noted, a defense program got underway in mid-1940. For a time, it was possible simultaneously to expand the output of both civilian and military goods. This dual expansion clearly could not continue past the point of full employment. In fact, the output of some types of consumer goods (e.g., aluminum products) virtually ceased long before this point was reached, and by late 1941 or early 1942 additional output of war materials generally could be obtained only by the sacrifice of civilian goods production.

The labor market tightened as production expanded and as potential workers were drawn into the armed forces. Competition for labor could have produced an immense explosion in the rate of increase in money wages. In fact, average hourly earnings in manufacturing

(Table 7.3) did increase by 36 percent between 1939 and 1942 and by an additional 12 percent between 1942 and 1943. These advances, however, were only partly accounted for by increases in wage rates; they reflected also such factors as increases in overtime and late-shift premium pay, and shifts in the composition of the work force from low- to high-wage occupations and industries.

In October 1942 a remarkably effective wage rate stabilization program began.[40] The tabulation below, which utilizes a special wartime index of wage rates, compares the movement of hourly earnings and wage rates in manufacturing for selected periods from January 1941 to September 1947.[41]

Index of Average Hourly Earnings and Wage Rates in Manufacturing,
January 1941–September 1947   (January 1941=100)

Period	Hourly Earnings	Wage rates
January 1941	100.0	100.0
October 1942	130.7	117.0
August 1945	149.9	133.9
September 1947	183.2	174.4

It will be noted that during the prestabilization period (January 1941–October 1942) average hourly earnings in manufacturing increased about 31 percent, as compared with a 17 percent increase in wage rates. From October 1942 to the end of the war (August 1945), the increase in the two indexes was about the same (roughly 14 percent). During the industrial reconversion period to September 1947, during which wage controls were lifted and more normal patterns of industrial employment and hours of work were restored, the advance in wage rates was 30 percent and in hourly earnings 22 percent.

Consumer prices rose by 19 percent between 1939 and 1942, and advanced another 6 percent between 1942 and 1943. Price control and consumer goods rationing, reinforced by wage control, a remarkably high rate of savings, and sharp increases in personal and corporate income taxes, secured a substantially stable price level over the years 1943–45. With the end of the war and the dismantling of controls, consumer prices shot up between 1945 and 1947 by 24 percent.

Because of price controls, rationing, and the virtual disappearance of some types of consumer goods, the measurement of real wages during the war period has little meaning. A comparison of the position of workers in 1939 with that in 1947 has greater significance. Thus, factory workers appear to have been decidedly better off in the latter year, their real average hourly earnings having increased by about 19 percent. On the other hand, the union wage scales of building trades workers, in real terms, were lower by 10 percent, and the average annual salaries of teachers by 17 percent.

Over the whole period from 1900 to 1947, the real average hourly earnings of factory workers almost tripled, rising at an average annual rate of 2.4 percent. Teachers did somewhat less well, their average salaries increasing at an average annual rate of 1.9 percent. The average annual rate of increase in union scales in building over the somewhat shorter period 1907–47 was 1.7 percent.

The Period 1947–78

In terms of labor compensation, the period following World War II was extraordinary and, in some ways, puzzling. Between 1947 and 1978, real wages and living standards rose sharply, but the rate of increase in real terms declined markedly during the latter part of the period. Fringe benefits expanded rapidly, as shown in Chapter 2, and became an important part of the wage bargain in both the union and nonunion sectors. Collective bargaining in many strategic sectors of the economy became institutionalized, but the advance of trade unionism in relation to employment in nonfarm establishments reached a peak in 1954 and slowly declined thereafter. The long-term collective bargaining contract became commonplace. In various forms, the cost-of-living escalator clause made its appearance in union agreements, its coverage tending to fluctuate with changes in the movement of consumer prices. There was a growth of professionalism in wage negotiation and administration on both the management and union sides, which had its roots in wartime experience with wage controls and in the increasingly complex nature of wage decisions.

With the end of the war in 1945, the conversion to peacetime production was accomplished with surprising ease and rapidity. There were, of course, serious problems of readjustment for many industrial firms and for large numbers of workers. But the mass unemployment widely predicted for the immediate postwar period failed to materialize, due to the huge volume of liquid assets accumulated during the war and the severe war-induced shortages of many types of consumer goods. The federal government was given a positive role in the maintenance of output and employment at relatively high levels by the passage by the Congress of the Employment Act of 1946. During the years that followed, the economic advisory machinery set up under that act became increasingly important in the development of governmental policies calculated to foster employment and economic growth.[42]

The output of goods and services expanded enormously during the years following the end of the war. The gross national product in terms of dollars of constant purchasing power almost tripled between 1947 and 1978. The expansion was not uninterrupted. The period was marked by recessions in business activity in 1948–49, 1953–54, 1957–58, 1960–61, 1970–71, and 1973–75. Recovery to and expansion beyond previous cyclical peaks was comparatively swift, although the 1973–75 recession was considerably more severe than the earlier downturns. Over the entire period, output grew at an average annual rate of 3.6 percent.

The growth in output reflected, in part, growth in the labor force and in employment. The civilian labor force 16 years of age and over increased from 59.4 million in 1947 to 100.4 million in 1978, or by 69 percent. The increase in employment (57 million in 1947 to 94.4 million in 1978) was not quite proportionate.[43] There were marked changes in employment by industry and occupation. Employment increased by about 31 percent in manufacturing and by 17 percent in transportation and public utilities, but more than tripled in the service industries and almost so in government (mainly state and local), and about doubled in trade and in construction. It fell by approximately 12 percent in mining. Agricultural employment continued its long secular decline, falling from an average of 7.9 million in 1947 to 3.3 million in 1978, or by about 58 percent.

In the analysis of changes in money and real wages, it is not inappropriate to divide the postwar period into two parts: 1947–66 and 1966–78. By 1966, our involvement in Vietnam had assumed major proportions; at the same time, a variety of domestic social programs were being inaugurated or expanded. These events triggered an inflation which became a continuing and pervasive problem. Moreover, the social costs of industrial output began to receive increased attention, and, notably with Mishan's powerful polemic in 1967, the desirability of economic growth itself was called into question.[44] In ways difficult to measure, the operation of the labor market was affected by antidiscrimination hiring and promotion programs designed for minority groups and women, and to some extent by changing attitudes toward work. Beginning in late 1973, the impact of the OPEC oil cartel had marked effects on an energy-intensive society.

Table 7.4 shows indexes in money and real terms of average hourly earnings, adjusted for overtime premium pay (manufacturing only) and interindustry employment shifts, for production or nonsupervisory workers in the private nonfarm economy. The labor force coverage of this measure is comprehensive—about 57.5 million workers in 1978. Moreover, it provides a rough indication of change in the level of wage rates.[45] Also shown in Table 7.4 are indexes of money and real general wage rate changes effective in major union contracts (those covering 1,000 workers or more) for the 1966–78 period. Unfortunately, these data do not extend back to 1947. A discussion of some important aspects of wage developments which seem to differentiate the postwar years from earlier periods is reserved for Chapter 8.

Over the whole period from 1947 to 1978, the adjusted average hourly earnings of the basic nonfarm work force increased at an average annual rate of 5.3 percent. After taking account of the increase in the prices of consumer goods and services, the advance in real terms was at an average annual rate of 1.7 percent.

The rates of increase were distinctly different for the two sub-periods, 1947–66 and 1966–78. During the former period, the level of adjusted hourly earnings advanced at average annual rates of 4.3 percent in money and 2.3 percent in real terms. During the latter period, money wages increased at an average annual rate of almost 7 percent, but of only 0.9 percent in terms of purchasing power. As measured by general wage rate changes, workers under major union agreements fared somewhat better during 1966–78 than all workers in the private nonfarm economy, but not strikingly so. Money wages for the union workers increased at an average annual rate of 7.1 percent; the annual rate of increase in real terms was 1.1 percent.

In neither of the two postwar subperiods, of course, was the rate of change consistent from year to year. This is shown clearly by Table 7.5, where year-to-year percentage changes in the level of adjusted

Table 7.4. Indexes of Money and Real Adjusted Average Hourly Earnings in Private Nonfarm Economy, General Wage Changes in Major Union Contracts, and Consumer Prices, 1947–78 (1967=100)

Year	Adjusted† average hourly earnings, private nonfarm economy‡		General wage changes effective in major union contracts*		Consumer prices
	Money	Real	Money	Real	
1947	42.6	63.7			66.9
1948	46.0	63.8			72.1
1949	48.2	67.5			71.4
1950	50.0	69.3			72.1
1951	53.7	69.0			77.8
1952	56.4	70.9			79.5
1953	59.6	74.4			80.1
1954	61.7	76.6			80.5
1955	63.7	79.4			80.2
1956	67.0	82.3			81.4
1957	70.3	83.4			84.3
1958	73.2	84.5	75.0	86.6	86.6
1959	75.8	86.8	77.6	88.9	87.3
1960	78.4	88.4	80.1	90.3	88.7
1961	80.8	90.2	82.3	91.9	89.6
1962	83.5	92.2	84.6	93.2	90.6
1963	85.9	93.7	87.1	95.0	91.7
1964	88.3	95.1	89.4	96.2	92.9
1965	91.6	96.9	92.5	97.9	94.5
1966	95.4	98.1	95.8	98.6	97.2
1967	100.0	100.0	100.0	100.0	100.0
1968	106.2	101.9	105.5	101.2	104.2
1969	113.2	103.1	110.9	101.0	109.8
1970	120.7	103.8	118.7	102.1	116.3
1971	129.2	106.5	128.2	105.7	121.3
1972	137.5	109.7	135.9	108.5	125.3
1973	146.0	109.7	145.8	109.5	133.1
1974	157.5	106.6	159.5	108.0	147.7
1975	170.7	105.8	173.4	107.6	161.2
1976	183.0	107.3	187.4	109.9	170.5
1977	196.8	108.4	202.4	111.5	181.5
1978	212.6	108.9	219.0	112.1	195.3
Average annual rate of increase:					
1947–78	5.3	1.7			3.5
1947–66	4.3	2.3			2.0
1966–78	6.9	0.9	7.1	1.1	6.0

Source: U.S. Department of Labor, Bureau of Labor Statistics

† Adjusted for overtime payments (manufacturing only) and for interindustry employment shifts.

‡ Production of nonsupervisory workers.

* Contracts affecting 1,000 workers or more.

Table 7.5. Year-to-Year Percentage Changes in Money and Real Adjusted Average Hourly Earnings, Private Nonfarm Economy, and Consumer Prices, 1947–78

Year	Adjusted average hourly earnings*		Consumer prices
	Money	Real	
1947–48	8.0	0.2	7.8
1948–49	4.8	5.8	−1.0
1949–50	3.7	2.7	1.0
1950–51	7.4	−0.5	7.9
1951–52	5.0	2.8	2.2
1952–53	5.7	4.9	0.8
1953–54	3.5	3.0	0.5
1954–55	3.2	3.6	−0.4
1955–56	5.2	3.7	1.5
1956–57	4.9	1.3	3.6
1957–58	4.1	1.4	2.7
1958–59	3.5	2.7	0.8
1959–60	3.4	1.8	1.6
1960–61	3.1	2.1	1.0
1961–62	3.3	2.2	1.1
1962–63	2.9	1.7	1.2
1963–64	2.8	1.5	1.3
1964–65	3.7	2.0	1.7
1965–66	4.1	1.3	2.8
1966–67	4.8	1.9	2.9
1967–68	6.2	1.9	4.2
1968–69	6.6	1.2	5.3
1969–70	6.6	0.7	5.9
1970–71	7.0	2.6	4.3
1971–72	6.4	3.0	3.3
1972–73	6.2	0.0	6.2
1973–74	7.9	−2.8	11.0
1974–75	8.4	−0.7	9.1
1975–76	7.2	1.3	5.7
1976–77	7.5	1.0	6.5
1977–78	8.0	0.5	7.6

Source: U.S. Department of Labor, Bureau of Labor Statistics.

* Production or nonsupervisory workers; adjusted for overtime payments (manufacturing only) and interindustry employment shifts.

hourly earnings for nonfarm workers and for consumer prices are set forth. For the 1947–66 period, the annual change in the level of money wages ranged from 2.8 percent (1963–64) to 8.0 percent (1947–48); the annual change in real wages varied from −0.5 percent (1950–51) to 5.8 percent (1948–49). During 1966–78, the annual change in money wages ranged from 4.8 percent (1966–67) to 8.2 percent

(1974–75); in real terms, the range was from −2.8 percent (1973–74) to 3.0 percent (1971–72).

The major gains in real wages during the first part of the postwar period occurred during periods of substantial price stability, notably 1948–50 and 1951–56. When prices moved upward, as in 1956–58, the rate of real wage increase tended to fall. During the second part of the period, the gain in real wages took place between 1966 and 1972; in fact, real rates of pay, as measured by the adjusted average hourly earnings index, actually declined between 1972 and 1978.

The fact must be emphasized that during the postwar period the rate of increase in labor compensation, which included employer expenditures on fringe benefits, appears to have been greater than the indexes in Table 7.4 indicate for hourly wages alone. This was suggested by the data and related discussion in Chapter 2 of the rise of supplementary benefits as a component of compensation. For the postwar period as a whole, there is no satisfactory statistical series for production and nonsupervisory workers that shows the combined effect of changes in wage rates and employer expenditures on benefits. For production workers in manufacturing, such data were shown in Table 2.2 for the 15-year period 1959–74. For that period, the average annual increase in total compensation *per hour worked* was 5.6 percent, as compared with 5.0 percent in direct wages.

In terms of the factors affecting the trend of money and real rates of pay, there are two outstanding differences between the two subperiods into which the postwar years have been divided.

During 1947–66, the Consumer Price Index increased at an average annual rate of only 2.0 percent; the average rate of increase during 1966–78 was 6.0 percent. The inflationary episodes during the first part of the period were of short duration; the rise in the level of prices after 1966, on the other hand, represents the longest inflationary period in our history and at this writing (1979) the end is not in sight. Some of the consequences of this development are discussed in the following chapter.

The second major difference between the two subperiods is found in productivity experience. Between 1947 and 1966, the average annual rate of increase in output per hour of all persons in the private business sector was 3.3 percent. This rate was cut in half—to 1.6 percent—over the years 1966–78. The reasons for this slowdown in the rate of growth are complex, as indicated earlier in this chapter in the section on productivity. The point here simply is that the trend in productivity since 1966 largely explains the relatively small rate of increase in real wages experienced by the working population during 1966–78 as compared with the earlier part of the postwar period.

Selected Readings

Most of the principal sources for the movement of money and real wages in the United States are indicated by the text references. A major additional source is E. H. Phelps Brown and Margaret H. Browne's *A Century of Pay* (New York: St. Martin's Press, 1968), a comparative study of wages, prices, and productivity from 1860 to 1960 in five countries, including the United States. Some possible conclusions from the record are advanced in section 4 of this study. A paper by Albert Rees, "Patterns of Wages, Prices and Productivity," in *Wages, Prices, Profits, and Productivity* (New York: American Assembly, Columbia University Press, 1959), edited by Charles A. Myers, contains an analysis of some factors affecting the behavior of real wages over the period 1889–1957.

On the meaning and significance of productivity, see John W. Kendrick's *Understanding Productivity: An Introduction to the Dynamics of Productivity Change* (Baltimore: Johns Hopkins University Press, 1977). A review of post-World War II productivity experience and some cautious short-term projections will be found in Ronald E. Kutscher, Jerome A. Mark, and John R. Norsworthy's "The Productivity Slowdown and the Outlook to 1985," *Monthly Labor Review*, May 1977.

8

Rising Expectations and General Wage Changes: The Postwar Years

As the preceding chapter indicates, the American experience, almost from the beginning, has fostered expectations of gains in real wages, and hence in living standards, among the working population. The available statistics indicate that in most periods the economy has yielded rising real rates of pay. Impressive gains in leisure also have been achieved through reduction in standard hours of work and, in recent decades, through provision for paid vacations and holidays. Increases in real wages generally have come about through rising money rates coupled, especially during the nineteenth century, with essentially stable or falling prices. Inflation, even during the twentieth century, has been episodic, at least until recent years. The trend of productivity, an essential ingredient of real wage advance, has been generally upward. A number of factors have contributed to this result, and have enabled a portion of the productivity gains to be captured in wages despite large increases in labor supply.

Until the period following World War II, these expectations were, in a sense, unstructured. That is, gains in money and real wages largely were achieved through the operation of unorganized labor markets. Money wages reflected what employers needed to pay to recruit and retain an adequate labor force; they tended to change, sometimes downward, as market conditions altered. A union presence could affect the timing and sometimes the size of adjustments. But even in the comparatively small unionized sector, wage expectations were not tied to annual or other periodic adjustments, but were more general and long term in character.

The Rise of Wage Expectations

For a variety of reasons, expectations of periodic, usually annual, gains in money (and real) wages began to form during the years following World War II. This was a striking development that has been little noticed, at least until recently. It had its roots in at least four factors: (1) the consolidation after the war of union organization and collective bargaining in many sectors of the economy; (2) despite six recessions, the general prosperity and relatively high level of employment of the postwar years; (3) the greatly expanded role of the federal government in the management of the economy, which was accompanied by the growth of statistical systems that provided infinitely more, and more timely, information on output, employment, wages, prices, and other economic magnitudes than had hitherto been available;[1] and finally, (4) the upward creep in the general price level, and since 1966 a sustained inflation of unprecedented duration.

It was under these circumstances that by the 1970s expectations of periodic gains in wages became at least partially institutionalized. Workers began to perceive such gains as accruing at regular intervals. This expectation had been formalized, perhaps at the time fortuitously, in the celebrated 1948 contract between General Motors (GM) and the United Automobile Workers. This two-year agreement provided for an annual three-cent an hour wage increase (about 2 percent), together with a cost-of-living escalator clause to assure the GM worker, in the words of the company, "that the buying power of his hour of work will increase as the Nation's industrial efficiency improves."[2]

The long-term collective bargaining agreement, defined as a contract extending for two years or more, was a social invention of considerable importance. It spread with comparative rapidity. By 1976, only 4.7 percent of major collective bargaining agreements, accounting for 3.5 percent of the workers covered by such contracts, were of less than two years' duration.[3] The average duration of major settlements reached during 1977 was 32.5 months.[4] The long-term contract typically provides for an annual increase in rates of pay; if accompanied by an escalator clause, additional adjustments may take place at quarterly, semiannual, or annual intervals, depending on the escalator provisions and the behavior of consumer prices.

Annual pay adjustments as a matter of personnel policy also have become common in the private nonunion sector of the economy. These may reflect considerations of equity, the influence of union settlements, and problems of worker retention and recruitment. In government, a notable action was the Federal Salary Reform Act of 1962, which provided for the annual review of federal salary scales for white-collar workers and for annual pay adjustments, subject to executive branch recommendations and congressional action. For federal blue-collar workers, annual pay review had long been provided for by other legislation.

Expectations of regular gains in money and real wages were strengthened by the promulgation in 1962 of noninflationary guideposts to wage (and price) increases by the Council of Economic Advisers.[5] The guideposts tied increases in money wages to the trend rate of productivity in the national economy. The accompanying discussion of pay policy undoubtedly broadened anticipations of annual wage gains. The prolonged inflation beginning in 1966, which led to mandatory wage-price controls during the first part of the 1970s and a new set of wage-price guideposts in 1978, gave added stimulus to annual pay adjustments, often supplemented in union agreements by cost-of-living escalator arrangements.

Phelps Brown reminds us that each year a smaller proportion of the labor force can remember the 1930s when money wage behavior was conditioned, firm by firm or industry by industry, by its effect on costs, prices, and employment. The general prosperity of the postwar period has largely removed the fear of joblessness from major segments of the labor force, and, for employers, has loosened pricing restraints that existed under tighter product market conditions. This means for the worker that

> the old inhibition against rocking the boat will have been replaced by a heightened awareness of bargaining power and a sense of security from the risk of over-reaching oneself. At the same time the cumulative rise of money wages and of prices will have dissolved old notions of the significance of the unit of money, and substituted new notions of

magnitude, and a sense that the purchasing power of money is something that is always falling. A cumulative rise in the standard of living of manual workers will have brought many into a region where some further rise will afford not some quantitative increase merely, but a new way of life, and be demanded with a corresponding intensity. It may also be a general rule that when the objective standard of living rises progressively, the subjective rises even faster: a gap opens between what we have now and what we feel we are entitled to expect: we have never been so prosperous and never so discontented. If differentials, again, are maintained percentage-wise, then as the general level rises the absolute difference between the low paid and the average widens until it appears indefensible; but when the lower paid are brought up, the others are powerfully moved to restore their differentials. All these developments have tended to detach expectations about the attainable rise in pay from the current state of the economy.[6]

Phelps Brown was writing with British conditions particularly in view, but his analysis, as he points out, has wide application among industrial countries. Expectations, shaped by a variety of factors that have conditioned postwar economic development, clearly play a role in the fashioning of the contours of general changes in money wages. This factor may help to explain why in the United States money wages rose about as rapidly during the 1970–71 recession as during the expansion phase of the cycle.[7] During the first four postwar recessions, the rate of increase in money wages had declined markedly. Again, the sharp recession beginning in the fall of 1973—the sixth recession during the postwar period—had no decisive effect on the rate of wage increase, despite the fact that the national unemployment rate rose to 8.5 percent during 1975. In major collective bargaining settlements, for example, first-year general wage rate increases averaged 5.8 percent in 1973, 9.8 percent in 1974, 10.2 percent in 1975, and then declined moderately to 8.4 percent in 1976 and 7.8 percent in 1977. The decline in 1977 has been attributed to greater emphasis on fringe benefit improvements.[8]

Diversity in Wage Settlements

The postwar forces in the United States that have led to widespread expectations of annual gains in money wages have not resulted in uniform rates of increase. These expectations must be filtered through

97

the labor market, that immensely complex mechanism through which the wage level is determined by thousands upon thousands of collective and individual bargains and employer personnel actions.

The process of wage determination in the United States remains highly decentralized. The wages and salaries of more than two-thirds of the nonfarm labor force are arrived at through unilateral employer action. Moreover, collective bargaining within the unionized sector is itself relatively decentralized as compared, for example, with Great Britain or Sweden.

The average rate of increase in wages that occurs over a period of time, conventionally a year, depends largely upon a complex of factors operating in the labor market or, more accurately, in the numerous submarkets where wage determination for most types of employees actually occurs. An individual wage decision will in some measure reflect conditions specific to the particular firm or industry, including conditions in the labor and product markets in which the firm or industry operates. Unemployment rates (as indicators of labor market conditions) and levels and rates of change in profits (as indicative of the state of the product market) are relevant. A marked upward trend in consumer prices, say at an annual rate of 2 percent or more, will tend to operate as a general factor in wage adjustment. Institutional factors, of which trade unionism and employer organizations are most noteworthy, also have an important role to play.

As Hildebrand has strongly emphasized, *general* movements in productivity or employment have little influence, for the most part, on *particular* wage decisions. "Because our system of collective bargaining is so decentralized," he writes, "it is much more responsive to economic factors local to the bargaining zone—profit prospects of the employers and employment-unemployment in the particular industry or trade. The exception here is overall movements of the cost of living, which, unlike the national unemployment rate or the trend advance in general labor productivity, have real and understandable significance to union members everywhere."[9]

Despite strong expectations of annual wage adjustments and the influence of a prolonged rise in the level of consumer prices, considerable diversity in wage decisions continues to exist. This is shown, for example, by the data on settlements in major collective bargaining situations reported in *Current Wage Developments,* published monthly by the Bureau of Labor Statistics. These major agreements, in turn, are not necessarily representative of settlements for workers (about half the total union membership) under smaller contracts, nor for the much larger nonunion component of the labor force.

The Inflation Factor in Wage Decisions

As previously indicated, *general* movements in productivity, for the most part, have little explicit role in wage decisions in a decentralized system of wage determination. For particular firms or industries, increasing productivity may have a significant bearing on profitability, which may well influence wage decisions in these situations. The secular increase in productivity, taking the economy as a whole, is a major source of expansion in the demand for labor and in this sense may condition the climate within which money wage determination occurs.[10]

The situation is rather different with general changes in the cost of living. A strong upward movement in the level of retail prices is felt by wage earners and their families everywhere, and a wage response is almost inevitable. This response will take a variety of forms, and its strength will depend in part on the magnitude of the price rise and on expectations with respect to future change.

Although not strictly a cost-of-living index, the monthly Consumer Price Index (CPI) prepared by the Bureau of Labor Statistics is almost universally used for that purpose. Like any general index, the CPI is an abstraction. For any given family, a change in costs for an equivalent level of living from one period to another rarely will correspond with the change in the index. There are three principal reasons. One is that consumption patterns differ substantially among family units, due to differences in size, age, taste, income, and other characteristics. A second is that a given change in the index may relate, at least in part, to index components (e.g., home financing charges) the prices of which are fixed over long periods for many families. The third is that the substitution of goods or services yielding roughly equivalent satisfaction may be possible for at least some of those that have changed in price.

These considerations suggest that the effect of small changes in the index (say a monthly rise of one-tenth of an index point) differs widely among consumer units and is not felt in a general way by the working population, at least in the short run. If this is the case, little wage pressure will be generated, except under escalator clauses that are tied to small changes in the CPI. When price changes are small, the main sources of wage pressure must be sought in the behavior of other "explanatory variables," such as demand-supply conditions in the labor market and profits.

It is when the upward movement of prices quickens, and extends substantially throughout the whole range of consumer goods and services, that wages begin to respond directly to price movements. Experience during the 1960s is instructive. Between 1960 and 1965, the CPI rose at an average annual rate of about 1.3 percent, with more than half of the increase, over the period as a whole, accounted for by services. Between 1965 and 1966, the increase jumped to almost 3 percent, with the advance extending to most of the index components. The average cost of food consumed at home, which is especially critical in terms of housewife reaction, rose by 5 percent. By mid-1966, rising prices had become an explicit factor in wage determination. This was shown by the adoption of cost-of-living escalator clauses in several important collective bargaining contracts, and by a general rise in the size of wage increases. It should be noted that the upsurge in prices came in conjunction with other factors exerting pressure on the wage level at that time, particularly a tightening of the labor market as reflected in the national unemployment rate.

A sustained rise in the level of consumer prices will be reflected in a variety of ways in collectively bargained wage settlements. In some situations, where money wages have lagged the rise in prices, "catch-up" adjustments may be incorporated in the agreements. This appears to have occurred, for example, in the 1976 settlements at major companies in the rubber industry, where a large initial wage increase in three-year contracts was granted after extensive strike activity. Much smaller increases were agreed to for the second and third years, together with a cost-of-living escalator clause that had not been part of the previous contracts.[11]

Agreements also may reflect anticipated increases in the cost of living. This surely helps to explain why general wage changes typically are larger in major agreements without escalator clauses. Thus, in major contract settlements in 1977, the average rate of change in wages over the life of the contract was almost 7 percent for contracts without escalator provisions as compared to 5 percent for contracts with such clauses.[12] Average contract duration was shorter in the absence of escalator arrangements.

The prolonged inflation beginning in 1966 had a decisive influence on the adoption of cost-of-living escalator clauses in major collective bargaining agreements. Of the 10 million workers under major contracts in manufacturing and nonmanufacturing industries as of January 1966, about 2 million, or 20 percent, were covered by escalator clauses. At the beginning of 1978, 5.8 million, about 60 percent of the 9.7 million workers then under major agreements, had such coverage. In addition, it was estimated on the basis of survey data that approximately 900,000 workers under smaller union contracts in manufacturing and 125,000 workers in nonunion manufacturing plants also were covered by formal escalator arrangements.[13] Hard estimates are not available for the escalator coverage of workers under small union contracts in nonmanufacturing industries or in government employment. Crude estimates suggest that these two segments may account roughly for 1.8 million workers under escalation. Total worker coverage under formal escalator plans, therefore, was in the neighborhood of 8.6 million at the beginning of 1978, or about 10.5 percent of those on nonfarm payrolls.

An escalator clause imposes a contractual obligation upon an employer to change rates of pay in accordance with a formula embodied in a collective bargaining agreement. Such clauses are found largely in contracts of three-year duration. Substantial differences exist among arrangements for wage escalation in American industry. As a product of collective bargaining, escalator clauses tend to be related to other terms agreed upon by unions and employers in specific wage settlements. The most important variations among escalator provisions are those relating to the timing of cost-of-living reviews, the formula for determining escalator adjustments in pay, and the limitations, if any, upon the size of such adjustments.

Escalator pay adjustments rarely compensate completely for the increase in living costs. Special tabulations by the Bureau of Labor Statistics for 1973 and 1974 provide distributions by size of increase of workers under major agreements with escalator clauses effective during the entire calendar year.[14] In 1973, the increase in the CPI was 8.8 percent. About 20 percent of the 4 million workers under major agreements with escalator provisions received no increase, mainly because their contracts provided for no cost-of-living review during the year. About 68 percent of the workers who received escalator adjustments received increases of either 4 and under 5 percent, or 5 and under 6 percent. Contracts in the transportation equipment industry generally fell in the 4 and under 5 percent interval, with communications in the 5 and under 6 percent group. About 22 percent of the workers received increases of less than 4 percent; at the upper end of the distribution, increases of 6 percent or more went to 9 percent of the workers. For the 80 percent of the workers under major agreements receiving escalator increases in 1973, the average was 4.3 percent.

In 1974, when the level of consumer prices advanced by 12.2 percent, the distribution of workers by escalator increases differed considerably from that for 1973. At the upper end of the distribution, about 29 percent of the 4.4 million workers under major agreements with escalator clauses, mainly in transportation equipment and basic steel, received increases of 9 and under 10 percent, and an additional 7 percent received increases of 10 percent or more. On the other hand, about 31 percent of the workers, heavily concentrated in local cartage and over-the-road trucking, obtained increases of less than 2 percent. About 14 percent of the workers fell in the 8 and under 9 percent interval. Approximately 26 percent of the workers received no escalator adjustment during the year. For those workers receiving escalator increases, the average in 1974 was 5.9 percent.

Data are available for a longer period, beginning with 1968, on the average increase received by workers under escalator clauses in major agreements. These are shown in Table 8.1 for the period 1968–77, together with the ratios of these average increases to increases in the level of consumer prices.

The ratio of escalator wage increases to price increases varied substantially from year to year, but the average ratio for the whole 10-year period, and also for the high inflation years 1973–77, was less than 0.6. This means that the yield of escalator clauses to workers who received cost-of-living adjustments averaged somewhat less than 60 percent of the increase in the Consumer Price Index. In a most interesting article, Perna terms this ratio a measure of the "elasticity" of the response under escalator clauses of wages to consumer price increases.[15] Actually, the ratio as calculated gives no weight to those

Table 8.1. Ratio of Average Escalator Wage Increases for Workers under Major Collective Bargaining Agreements to Increases in Consumer Price Index, 1968–77

	Percentage increases		Ratio of average escalator increases to CPI increases
Year	Consumer Price Index*	Average escalator wage†	
1968	4.7	1.6	0.34
1969	6.1	1.6	0.26
1970	5.5	3.7	0.67
1971	3.4	3.1	0.91
1972	3.4	2.0	0.59
1973	8.8	4.1	0.47
1974	12.2	5.8	0.48
1975	7.0	4.8	0.68
1976	4.8	3.5	0.73
1977	6.8	3.9	0.57
1968–77	6.3	3.4	0.57
1973–77	7.9	4.4	0.59

Source: U.S. Department of Labor, Bureau of Labor Statistics.

* December to December.

† Average increases for those workers under escalator clauses actually receiving increases. Coverage includes contracts with escalator clauses effective only part of a calendar year.

workers under escalator clauses who failed to receive cost-of-living increases. At least in 1973 and 1974, as indicated above, this number was substantial. If those workers with zero increases are included in the calculation, the elasticity ratio, at least for 1973–74, was not far from 0.4.

It is important to notice that the formal escalation of wages on the basis of cost-of-living changes is rarely the sole element in a wage bargain. As of mid-1976, only 41 of 1,570 major collective bargaining contracts studied provided for wage adjustment on a cost-of-living basis only.[16] As emphasized earlier in this chapter, the expectation has developed in the postwar period of a continuous increase in real wages through frequent upward changes in money wages. Hence cost-of-living escalator clauses, where they appear, are designed to protect, at least in part, the value in real terms of negotiated changes in rates of pay rather than simply to preserve the value of existing wage standards.

There are a number of specific issues relating to wage escalation, such as its effect on occupational wage differentials. But one general question deserves at least brief mention here; namely, whether the operation of escalator clauses in collective bargaining agreements contributes to inflationary pressures in the economy.

In its 1967 *Annual Report,* the Council of Economic Advisers stated that "if all unions—and other groups in society—were to succeed in tying compensation to consumer prices, the arrangement would become a vast engine of inflation, which, once it began to roll, would continue to gain speed."[17] In this universal sense, wage escalation simply does not exist, even in the union sector. As indicated earlier, wage escalator clause coverage as of the beginning of 1978 appeared to extend to about one-tenth of the employees of all nonagricultural establishments, including the government.

We have seen also that there is little justification for the commonly held belief that escalator wage adjustments fully compensate for changes in the cost of living. In fact, escalator wage increases in recent years have compensated, on the average, for less than 60 percent of the increases in the Consumer Price Index. In some situations, of course, the compensation ratio has been much higher, and in others substantially lower.

Finally, the escalator clause is only one way in which changes in living costs are reflected in collectively bargained wage settlements. In the absence of provision for escalation, past increases in living costs, if at all substantial, are likely to prove an important element in the wage bargain. At the same time, an effort will be made to take anticipated increases in living costs into account. In the much larger nonunion sector of the economy, where formal escalator arrangements are rare, significant changes in living costs provide a powerful impetus for upward wage adjustment. Considerations of equity are no doubt important in this connection, together with the desire on the part of employers, if the labor market is firm, to sustain employee morale, minimize turnover, and forestall unionization.

These considerations are not intended to dismiss contractual escalator clauses as of little or no significance in the inflationary process. They do play a role, and that role may become more important in the future if the economy cannot be so managed as to avoid persistent rises in living costs. In that case, the use of formal escalation may continue to spread and to become firmly institutionalized, and escalator provisions may compensate more rapidly and completely than many now do for living cost changes.[18]

In general, the difficulty with cost-of-living wage escalation is twofold. The first is its automaticity. Wage increases cannot be fully anticipated, and may hit particular firms or industries at times when their capacity to meet higher costs has been impaired by product market developments. The second is that the winding down of such inflationary episodes as do occur may prove more difficult if escalation does in fact become more widespread and more sensitive to small changes in the price index. These considerations may have employment implications that unions and management need to take into account in the bargaining process.

Suggested Readings

The emergence of the multiyear collective bargaining agreement is analyzed by Joseph W. Garbarino in *Wage Policy and Long-Term Contracts* (Washington, D.C.: Brookings Institution, 1962). The characteristics of postwar wage bargaining are usefully summarized by George Rubin in "Major Collective Bargaining Developments—A Quarter Century Review," *Current Wage Developments,* February 1974.

An account of wage escalator clauses as one response to rising prices will be found in H. M. Douty's *Cost-of-Living Escalator Clauses and Inflation* (Washington, D.C.: Council on Wage and Price Stability, 1975). Victor J. Sheifer, in "Cost-of-Living Adjustment: Keeping Up with Inflation?" *Monthly Labor Review,* June 1979, discusses the factors determining the yield of escalator clauses.

9

Unions and the Wage Bargain

In 1930, the membership of unions in the United States (exclusive of Canadian membership) numbered about 3.4 million, or 11.6 percent of the employees in nonagricultural establishments. Membership increased rapidly during the latter part of the 1930s and during World War II, and in 1945 was placed at 14.3 million, or 35.5 percent of nonfarm establishment employment. Over the next three decades, union membership grew by an additional 5 million, but failed to keep pace with increasing employment. Union membership in 1976, the most recent year for which such data are available, accounted for only about one-fourth of nonfarm establishment employment. If the membership of employee associations with collective bargaining functions, such as the National Education Association, is added to union membership, the combined total in 1976 was 22.5 million, or about 28.3 percent of the employees of nonagricultural establishments.[1]

Clearly the wages and other conditions of employment of not much more than a quarter of the employees in nonfarm establishments in the United States are determined through the collective bargaining process. For several reasons, however, such a statement gives a misleading impression of its importance. It should be noted, first, that collective bargaining has become a basic labor market institution in many strategic sectors of the economy—in numerous manufacturing industries, in land, air, and water transportation, in communications and other public utilities, in mining, contract construction, and, in recent years, in important segments of public employment. Wage bargains in these sectors of output and employment not only have economic significance in their own right; they also have an influence on wage decisions in the larger nonunion segment.

A second consideration is that unions provide, however roughly, a mechanism for expressing the preferences of workers on the terms of wage settlements. The present-day complexity of the wage bargain, emphasized in Chapter 2, largely reflects the innovative tendencies of unions in the bargaining process. Thus, it is doubtful if, in the absence of union pressure, pension and medical insurance plans, paid for wholly or in part by employers, would have expanded with such astonishing rapidity for nonsupervisory workers during the postwar period. This expansion has extended, of course, to the nonunion sector.

In general, collective bargaining, once established, tends to be a continuous process, for unions are concerned with two aspects of the wage bargain. The first, which commands most public attention, relates to changes periodically in the basic terms of collective agreements. The second is the day-to-day application of these terms in the work place; that is, to wage administration. This latter function is by no means unimportant, for many problems relating to pay may arise during the term of an agreement.[2] The importance of unions in representing their members in the day-to-day problems that arise in the employment relationship, including administration of the non-economic terms of collective agreements, was stressed in Chapter 3. Our concern here, however, is primarily with the influence of unions on changes in the general level of pay.

The ability of unions to affect levels of pay rests in some sense on economic power. The question of power through organization does not exist in purely competitive labor markets, where neither the buyer nor the seller can influence the wage rate. But wage-setting through negotiation between unions and employers (or employer associations) introduces a new element, the role of bargaining, into the determination of rates of pay. Considerable attention has been devoted in recent decades to the theory of wage bargaining. Perhaps the most challenging effort in this direction has been made by the Dutch economist, Pen.[3]

Pen's theory deals with economic power and its application. The protagonists are the union as an institution and the representatives of the employer(s). Economic power arises out of the mutual dependence of the bargainers; that is, out of the "attachment" or interdependence of the parties. The concept of attachment involves the replaceability of the persons who comprise the work force. Attachment between the parties may be weak (as in a small unionized segment of a manufacturing industry) or strong (as in a highly unionized public utility). It is never absolute; it may be severed, since there is some wage rate at which substitution will occur or the exchange abandoned altogether. Granted some measure of attachment, a contract zone exists; within this zone, agreement between the bargainers is possible. But which wage rate within the contract zone will be agreed upon? Pen reduces his theory to a set of equations, one reflecting the position of the union leader and the other that of the employer. A determinate solution to the bargaining process is reached when both equations are satisfied at the same time.

Pen's theory is brilliant and elegant, but for several reasons his equations will not yield predictable results. Nevertheless, he has provided a more precise framework than we have had hitherto for analysis of the elements of the collective bargaining process. He has, for example, clarified such cloudy concepts as "bargaining power," and has provided new insights into union and employer valuations of the risk of conflict.

It is sufficient to note here that union bargaining power is conditioned by a variety of factors internal and external to the bargaining situation. Even in the most strongly unionized firms or industries, the power of unions to affect the level of wages is limited. However, unions that have achieved a measure of organization and employer recognition presumably possess some market power; that is, some ability to achieve and maintain rates of pay above the levels that would have existed in their absence.

But what is the magnitude of the union effect on wages? This is a difficult question, for we do not know what the wages of union workers would be in the absence of collective bargaining. It is necessary, therefore, to measure wage differences among groups of workers who are as comparable as possible except for the factor of unionization. The wage differentials that emerge, however, may fail to indicate fully the effects of unions, for nonunion employers often raise wages because unionized workers have won increases. This may be done in an effort to forestall unionization, or it may, in tight labor markets, be necessary to enable nonunion employers to compete for labor. Moreover, the wage effects of unions may be overestimated to the extent that relatively high-wage union employers are able to select and retain better qualified and more productive workers than lower-wage nonunion employers.

The most definitive study of union-nonunion wage differences remains that of Lewis.[4] Lewis examined and reworked a substantial number of studies of union wage effects, and contributed a careful analysis of data on wage trends in sectors of the private economy classified by extent of unionization. On the basis of his review of 20 studies of the impact of unionism on relative wages, some of which were done under his direction, Lewis concluded that, on the average, union wages exceeded nonunion levels by 15–20 percent in 1923–29; by more than 25 percent in 1931–33; by 10–20 percent in 1939–41; by 0–5 percent in 1945–49; and by 10–15 percent in 1957–58.[5] Another set of estimates, based on time series regressions prepared by Lewis, is broadly in line with those just cited.[6]

It will be noticed that Lewis' estimates of the relative effect of unionism vary substantially according to the time period. The union effect was greatest during the deep depression years of 1931–33, presumably a result of the downward wage rigidity in union contracts. The union effect declined during the partial economic recovery of the New Deal period beginning in 1933, and was almost wiped out during the inflationary and low unemployment years of World War II and its immediate aftermath. After 1950, the average differential of union over nonunion wages began to grow and reached 10–15 percent by 1957–58.

The study of Lewis was based on industry data. In the years that followed, a number of studies of union wage effects utilized new sources that provided data on the wages or earnings and union membership status of individual workers who could be classified, at least broadly, by industry and occupation and by such personal characteristics as sex, age, race, and education. An example of this type of analysis is provided by Boskin, who concluded, using 1967 data, that the magnitude of the union-nonunion wage differential varied by race, sex, location, and occupation, but was, on average, in line with the Lewis estimate of 10–15 percent for 1957–58.[7] Some other comparatively recent estimates based on individual worker data suggest somewhat higher union wage effects.[8] An average union wage effect of about 16 percent was found by Bloch and Kuskin using 1973 data.[9]

These figures may provide a corrective to exaggerated impressions of the power of unions to raise the wages of their members relative to those of nonunion workers. The figures shown are averages. The union effect will differ among industries and occupational groups. As we have seen, it varied at different times throughout the 1923–58 period covered by the Lewis study. It tended to be at a maximum during periods of falling prices and output, suggesting greater downward rigidity in union than in nonunion wages. In rising product and labor markets, on the other hand, the union-nonunion differential tended to fall, indicating again greater flexibility in wage adjustment in the nonunion sector.

A Bureau of Labor Statistics study of union-nonunion wage differentials in manufacturing indicates that such differentials narrowed during the 1960s, especially during the second half of the decade, and that "the narrowing coincides with the opinion of many economists that union wages are more rigid than nonunion wages during periods of large and unexpected demand-pull inflation."[10] The study indicates, however, that employer expenditures for fringe benefits rose more rapidly during this period for union than for nonunion workers, so that in terms of total compensation the union-nonunion ratio probably changed little.

Historically, inflationary episodes in the United States have been of short duration. In a prolonged inflation, such as that beginning in 1966, the tendency for increases in union rates of pay to lag advances in the nonunion sector may evaporate. Some evidence on this point is provided by occupationally based data on wage rate changes for workers in the private nonfarm economy published quarterly by the Bureau of Labor Statistics beginning in 1975.[11] This new series provides separate data for union and nonunion workers. Table 9.1 shows union-nonunion index series computed from these data.

At least over the short period from the third quarter of 1975 to the fourth quarter of 1978, Table 9.1 indicates that wage rate changes for union workers exceeded those for nonunion workers. The difference

Table 9.1. Indexes of Union and Nonunion Wage and Salary Rates, Private
Nonfarm Workers, by Quarter, 1975–78   (Third quarter
1975=100)

Year and quarter	Indexes of wage and salary rates	
	Union workers	Nonunion workers
1975		
III	100.0	100.0
IV	102.4	101.6
1976		
I	104.0	103.6
II	105.9	105.3
III	108.4	106.5
IV	110.6	108.4
1977		
I	112.1	110.0
II	114.6	111.9
III	116.8	113.8
IV	119.1	115.6
1978		
I	121.0	118.1
II	123.4	120.7
III	126.0	123.0
IV	128.5	124.4

Source: Computed from *Current Wage Developments,* October 1976, 1977, and 1978, and April 1979.

was not strikingly great—about 4 percentage points (3.3 percent) over the whole period. This result may mean, however, that unions, at least partly through wage escalator arrangements, have found ways to adjust rates of pay more quickly than in the past to sharp upward movements in prices.

To the extent that unions can exercise market power—that is, establish rates of pay above the level that would have prevailed under more competitive labor market conditions—their wage actions presumably have employment effects. These effects result from the use of additional capital in the form of labor-saving machinery and equipment or from higher product prices and hence reduction in the scale of output of the firm or industry, or from a combination of these factors. There are also other adjustments that firms can make to higher labor costs that have an impact on employment, such as the introduction of improved hiring standards designed, at least over the long run, to increase the level of worker quality and efficiency.

Such employment effects as arise from the imposition of union wage standards above the competitive level are rarely dramatic. They tend

111

to take place slowly as new equipment is installed, as output is transferred from high-cost to low-cost firms, as price effects are reflected in product demand, and as other adjustments occur. The effects may be masked in an expanding economy by the maintenance of employment in absolute terms in the union sector, or by a slower rate of growth than otherwise would have occurred.

Unfortunately, there is little quantitative evidence on the employment effects of wage bargaining. An example often cited relates to the bituminous coal industry, where output per hour of production workers more than tripled between 1947 and 1967.[12] Part of this gain in productivity no doubt would have taken place in any event through autonomous investment in improved technology, but to a considerable extent it seems to reflect rapid growth in the use of labor-saving techniques, including expansion in strip mining where labor costs are relatively small, in response to sharply rising wage rates. The reasons for the decline in coal mining productivity during the 1970s are not clear.

In general, the employment effects of wage bargains that establish rates of pay appreciably above competitive levels are most likely to be observed in situations in which substantial nonunion competition exists in product and labor markets. Palmer's fascinating case studies in the early 1930s of the experience of three textile unions in the Philadelphia area can still be read with profit.[13] Schultz and Myers studied wage determination in the shoe industry and in a New England textile community as part of a broader analysis of employment in relation to union wage decisions.[14] They concluded that, except in periods of full employment and rising prices, some unions tend to take into account the probably effect of wage demands on the level of employment of their members, particularly in industries where there is strong competition in the product market and where the industry is not completely organized. More recently, Henle has examined 12 situations in multiplant companies in which union contracts were reopened for renegotiation where management had announced that a particular operation or plant would be cut back, moved, abandoned, or sold.[15] Substantial changes in contract terms were made in most of these cases.

When low profitability in the airline industry in 1975–76 appeared to threaten serious employment curtailment, the unions concerned made substantial pay concessions in bargaining with some of the major carriers.[16] There are indications, to cite another case, that unions in the building industry in recent years have relaxed some working rules to improve the output of their members in the face of growing nonunion competition; at the same time, wage settlements have moderated.[17]

Mention should be made of the special case, which does not appear to have wide importance in the United States, in which the effect of union wage gains may, up to a point, increase employment in the union sector. This is the case in which the employer has a monopoly in the hiring of labor, and is usually called labor monopsony. It cannot be explained adequately without use of the technical expressions and graphic illustrations that adorn most textbooks in labor economics.[18] Put as simply as possible, in a monopsonistic situation an increase in wage rates, within limits, will have the paradoxical effect of increasing employment. The reason is that under monopsony the employer, by definition, is operating on an upward sloping labor supply curve (in contrast with an employer in a competitive labor market, where the supply curve to the individual firm is horizontal). Since the supply curve is imperfectly elastic, the marginal labor cost curve will lie above the supply curve. Hence the firm (or firms) will tend to employ less labor at a lower wage rate than in a relatively competitive labor market, and the value of the marginal labor product will tend to be higher. Under these conditions, the wage rate can be pushed up to the point at which it equals marginal value product with no adverse effect on employment; indeed, employment should increase. Above that point, however, employment will begin to decline as wages rise.

There has been a long controversy, unrelieved by much empirical data, over the extent to which monopsony is found in the American economy. Monopsony presupposes concentrations of employment in labor market areas each dominated by one or a small number of employers, or by effective collusive agreements among employers in an area on wage levels or wage increases. Neither of these conditions now seems to exist widely.[19] The automobile, in particular, has given new dimensions to worker mobility and has reduced labor market isolation, and the enforcement of collusive agreements in tight labor markets, where presumably such agreements have greatest appeal for employers, is fraught with the difficulties that beset most cartel arrangements.

In its economic goals, the mainstream of American trade unionism has always been highly pragmatic. It has not formulated its objectives in broad ideological terms.[20] Through collective bargaining, it has sought to maintain and advance the wage standards of its members within the bounds of the dynamics of American industry. It has exerted a measure of market power, varying with labor market conditions and among industries and occupational groups, and hence has raised, on the average, union as compared with nonunion wages. This probably has had some employment effect, reducing employment relatively in the union sector, and therefore affecting the composition of output in the economy. The outcome of collective bargaining has indirect effects on nonunion wages. Unions provide, however imperfectly, a mechanism through which workers can express their preferences in the wage bargain as between changes in rates of pay and the introduction or liberalization of supplementary benefits, including leisure.

Suggested Readings

The most recent U.S. Bureau of Labor Statistics publication on trade union structure and membership is its Bulletin 2044, *Directory of National Unions and Employee Associations, 1977* (Washington, D.C.: GPO, 1979).

An interesting approach to the question of union power and its exercise in collective bargaining that differs from that presented in the text will be found in Melvin W. Reder's "Job Scarcity and the Nature of Union Power," *Industrial and Labor Relations Review,* April 1960. See also J. R. Hicks's *The Theory of Wages,* 2d ed. (New York: St. Martin's Press, 1963), pp. 140–47 and 354–62.

The basic study by H. Gregg Lewis of the impact of unionism on relative wages, *Unionism and Relative Wages in the United States* (Chicago: University of Chicago Press, 1963), is highly technical, but something of its flavor and results can be obtained from chaps. 1 and 5. Studies of union-nonunion wage differences based on individual worker data are illustrated by Farrell E. Bloch and Mark S. Kuskin in, "Wage Determination in the Union and Nonunion Sectors," *Industrial and Labor Relations Review,* January 1978, and by Paul M. Ryscavage in, "Measuring Union-Nonunion Earnings Differentials," *Monthly Labor Review,* December 1974.

10

The Legal Minimum Wage and Employment

The introduction of a legal minimum wage, or an increase in an existing legal minimum rate, has consequences similar in some respects to a collective bargaining settlement that increases pay above the level that labor market forces, in the absence of unionism, would have generated. By definition, an increase in a legal minimum wage is not a general wage increase, for it affects directly only those workers whose rates of pay were below the new minimum. It may, however, affect indirectly the rates of workers already at or above the minimum, especially over some period of time. The impact of a rise in the minimum wage on wages and employment depends on a variety of factors, including the magnitude of the rise, the elasticity of the demand for labor in the employments affected by the minimum, the state of the product and labor markets, and the size of the employment sector not covered by the minimum wage action.

In the United States, minimum wage legislation first appeared at the state level beginning in 1912. This legislation, which took several forms, applied only to women and minors. The general criteria used in its application were the needs of a self-supporting woman. By 1923, minimum wage laws were found in 15 States, the District of Columbia, and Puerto Rico. In that year, the United States Supreme Court held the District of Columbia minimum wage law unconstitutional. This and other legal decisions and rulings of state attorneys general effectively ended this phase of state minimum wage activity. There was a resurgence of interest in state minimum wage legislation during the depression of the 1930s, and its constitutionality was established in 1937 through a reversal by the Supreme Court of its 1923 decision. Thereafter, a considerable growth in such legislation occurred, and, beginning in 1939 in Connecticut, coverage began to be extended to men.[1]

The Federal Fair Labor Standards Act

Interest in minimum wage legislation today is largely, although not entirely, at the federal level. In 1938, as part of the outpouring of legislation associated with the New Deal, Congress passed the Fair Labor Standards Act, which had at the time only ambivalent support from organized labor.[2] The act established a minimum wage of 25 cents an hour effective October 24, 1938, rising automatically to 30 cents, a year later. The goal was to reach 40 cents an hour by 1945. An industry committee procedure was provided to expedite the achievement of the 40-cent minimum.

In addition to minimum wage standards, the act also provided for the establishment of a basic 40-hour week for covered employees, with premium pay for excess hours. This standard was reached at the end of the second year of the operation of the act and still obtains.

The course of wages during World War II made the 40-cent minimum rate effectively obsolete prior to 1945. In fact, that minimum standard was achieved for all covered workers during 1944.[3] The first major amendments to the act were passed in 1949. The minimum wage was increased from 40 to 75 cents an hour, effective January 1, 1950. Insofar as the continental United States was concerned, the industry committee procedure was abandoned. For the mainland, a uniform national minimum wage, which was indeed the goal of the initial act, became clear national policy.

Since 1949, minimum rates of pay under the Fair Labor Standards Act have been raised by a series of amendments in 1956, 1961, 1966, 1974, and 1977. Beginning in 1961, the coverage of the Act has been greatly expanded to include employees of relatively large enterprises in retail trade and service industries, local transit, construction, gasoline service stations, hospitals and nursing homes, hotels and restaurants, laundries, schools, domestic servants, and workers on large farms. As of January 1978, the coverage of the act was estimated

116

at approximately 52 million nonsupervisory employees. This expansion in coverage obviously has implications for the employment effects of minimum wage increases. The shrinkage of the noncovered sector, much of it relatively low wage, eliminates a route to alternative employment for workers who, for one reason or another, cannot qualify for employment at the legal minimum.

An attempt is made in Table 10.1 to summarize the changes in federal minimum wage standards during the postwar period. As previously noted, a 40-cent minimum, the original goal of the Fair Labor Standards Act, was reached before the end of World War II. The minimum was increased to 75 cents on January 1, 1950. By January 1, 1979, the minimum had almost quadrupled to $2.90, and will reach $3.35 two years later. The table also indicates roughly the relationship of the changing minimum on its effective dates to the general level of hourly earnings in the private nonfarm economy. The ratio ranges from about 48 to 59 percent. The ratio tends to fall, of course, between changes in the minimum as the general level of hourly earnings rises. The value of a given minimum in terms of purchasing power also falls as consumer prices increase between changes in the minimum. Over the whole period since 1950, however, the real value of the minimum wage has increased substantially. Thus, the increase in the minimum rate from $0.75 in January 1950 to $2.90 in January 1979 represented an increase in purchasing power of about 33 percent.

The Differential Impact of Minimum Wage Changes

The various increases in the federal minimum wage have been the subject of extensive consideration within the administration and the Congress. The 1977 amendments, for example, were adopted after about eight months of congressional debate with respect to their size and possible effects. The direct impact of changes in the federal minimum wage—that is, the aggregate effect on the wages of workers earning less than the minimum—has not been inconsequential. It has been estimated, for instance, that the minimum rates effective February 1, 1967 ($1.40 for workers previously covered by the Act and $1.00 for newly covered employees), added about $1.1 billion to the wage bill annually.[4] The direct addition to the wage bill of the $2.65 minimum effective January 1, 1978, has been estimated at $2.2 billion.[5] Over periods of time, an increase in the minimum wage in

117

Table 10.1. Postwar Minimum Wage Changes Under Fair Labor Standards Act for Mainland United States

Year of enactment	Effective date of minimum	Minimum rate	Average hourly earnings, private nonfarm economy*	Ratio: minimum wage to average hourly earnings, private nonfarm economy
1949	January 1, 1950	$0.75	$1.28	0.59
1956	March 1, 1956	1.00	1.80	0.56
1961	September 3, 1961	1.15†	2.14	0.54
	September 3, 1963	1.25	2.28	0.55
1966	February 1, 1967	1.40‡	2.63	0.53
	February 1, 1968	1.60	2.77	0.58
1974	May 1, 1974	2.00**	4.17	0.48
	January 1, 1975	2.10	4.40	0.48
	January 1, 1976	2.30	4.72	0.49
1977	January 1, 1978	2.65	5.49	0.48
	January 1, 1979	2.90	5.95***	0.49
	January 1, 1980	3.10		
	January 1, 1981	3.35		

Source: Congressional Acts in years noted; for average hourly earnings, private nonfarm economy, U.S. Bureau of Labor Statistics.

* Production and nonsupervisory workers. Only annual averages of hourly earnings available prior to 1964.

† For newly covered employees: $1.00 effective September 3, 1961; $1.15 effective September 3, 1964; $1.25 effective September 3, 1965.

‡ For new nonfarm coverage: $1.00 effective February 1, 1967, rising to $1.60 in four additional annual steps; farm coverage: $1.00 effective February 1, 1967, rising to $1.30 in two additional annual steps.

** For nonfarm employees covered in 1966 and 1974: $1.90 for period ending December 31, 1974, rising to $2.30 in three steps by January 1, 1977; for farm workers: $1.60 for period ending December 31, 1974, rising to $2.30 in four steps by January 1, 1977.

*** Preliminary.

relatively low-wage industries will have some effect on the wages of workers above the minimum, but these indirect effects are difficult to measure on any aggregate basis.

A statement of the aggregate direct impact of a rise in the minimum wage may tend to understate its significance, especially if expressed as a proportion of the total wage bill. Thus, the estimated $2.2 billion direct wage bill effect of the $2.65 rate amounted to about 0.4 percent of total payroll. This seems relatively quite small. But an increase in the minimum wage has a sharply differential impact among industries and geographic areas. Some industries (e.g., basic steel, automobile assembly, and many others) were not affected at all by the $2.65 rate. Others were heavily affected.

An example is the contract cleaning services industry surveyed in 24 metropolitan areas in July 1977 by the Bureau of Labor Statistics. Eight of these areas were located in the South. Among these areas, the proportion of workers earning $2.65 an hour or less ranged form 26.8 percent in Washington, D.C., to 80 percent or more in Atlanta, Baltimore, Houston, and Memphis, and exceeded 55 percent in the remaining three areas.[6] In Memphis, to cite a specific example, the addition to the wage bill required to bring contract cleaning employees earning elss than $2.65 up to that level was in the neighborhood of 12 percent. Even a few areas outside the South (e.g., Pittsburgh, St. Louis, Denver-Boulder) had substantial proportions of workers in contract cleaning earning less than $2.65 an hour in July 1977.

An example from the manufacturing sector is represented by the hosiery industry, which is located largely in the South. In July 1976, 35.2 percent of the workers making women's hosiery were earning less than $2.65 an hour; the proportion was almost as great, 34.2 percent, in mills primarily producing men's, boys', or children's seamless hosiery, or other hosiery products, such as women's anklets and socks.[7]

Regionally, the most marked effect of federal minimum wage legislation has been on the South. This is partly because of the concentration in the South of a variety of industries, particularly in manufacturing, in which wages tend to be relatively low wherever they are found. But a fundamental and pervasive factor is that the South for many years has been a region of relative labor surplus. It has provided labor for its own industries and agriculture and has, at the same time, contributed substantially through net migration during most of the period to the labor supply of other regions of the country. The region's relative labor surplus has been largely at the unskilled and semiskilled levels, and has exerted, despite migration, heavy and continuous pressure on job opportunities and wages within the region.

Wage differentials based on skill tend to be greater within the South than in the remainder of the country; this means, of course, that interregional differentials tend to vary inversely by occupational skill level. This tendency was noted half a century ago in a pioneering study by Heer, who observed:

> the difference in hourly earnings between the South and the rest of the country is apparently at a maximum in the case of common labor and shows a tendency to become progressively less with each advance in grade of skill. In the case of one or two highly skilled occupations it disappears entirely. This tendency is not particularly pronounced as regards industries in which differences in grades of skill are slight and in which advancement from one occupation to another is comparatively easy. It is strikingly evident, however, in industries in which there are broad differences in skill between various occupational groups and in which passage from one group to another is difficult.[8]

Given the underlying labor supply situation, labor and capital movements between the South and the rest of the country have been generally in the anticipated directions. But it is unlikely that the southern wage differential, particularly at the relatively unskilled level, will disappear in the near future.[9] This means that changes in the federal minimum wage will continue, on the whole, to have a heavier impact on the South than on the rest of the country. This is conspicuously true in view of the extensions of coverage beginning in 1961 to many industries with large components of relatively unskilled labor.

It is perhaps noteworthy that the 1977 amendments to the Fair Labor Standards Act included provision for an independent Minimum Wage Study Commission to examine a number of issues related to the minimum wage. One of the six questions posed to the commission is the employment, price, and indirect wage effects of minimum wages. This question alone is sufficient to test the analytical and expository talents of the commission and its staff, which must submit its final report to the president and the Congress within three years.

The Controversy over the Employment Effects of Minimum Wage Actions

Argument over the employment (and welfare) effects of minimum wage legislation are long-standing. For the most part, economists have contended that a legal minimum wage in competitive labor markets will have an adverse employment effect among workers whose contribution to output is worth less that the minimum. Stigler presented this position in a well-known paper in 1946.[10] The discharge of less efficient workers, he wrote, "will be larger the more the value of their services falls short of the legal minimum, the more elastic the demand for the product, and the greater the possibility of substituting other productive services (including efficient labor) for the inefficient workers' services." The result, in his view, was that at best the discharged workers would move into uncovered employments, where their wages would be lower; those not far below the minimum might have their wages raised to the minimum level. Unless the productivity of inefficient workers rises, aggregate output will be reduced.

The exception to this scenario was in the case of monopsony (see preceding chapter), which Stigler does not consider very relevant to the question of a national minimum wage. His reasons are that the "optimum" minimum (which under monopsony would tend to increase employment) must in the first place be correctly chosen, which presumes that labor demand and supply schedules are known over a considerable range; that the "optimum" minimum varies among occupations and, within an occupation, with the quality of worker; and that it varies among producing establishments and through time.

The proponents of minimum wage legislation tend to deny or minimize, at least within limits, the employment effects of a rise in the minimum wage standard. A clear statement of this position was by Lester in a controversy with Peterson.[11] Lester wrote that his position is that,

for a number of reasons, the orthodox model [of wage-employment effects] lacks good predictive value within a limited zone or range of wage change. Within such a range, the effects of a wage change imposed by a legal minimum wage can take any one of a variety of paths. Along some of those paths there may be no employment consequences or even some employment increases, provided the wage rise is moderate and within the range. A range of diverse reaction or latitude for nonemployment adjustment exists because (1) labor is not purchased and sold as the orthodox model postulates and, therefore, for the same grade of labor a significant band of wages prevails in a local market, including economically unjustified race, sex, and interfirm wage differences; (2) management often has flexibility and alternative means of adjustment so that it is not forced to confine its reaction within the wage-employment plane; (3) the process of labor and management adjustment to a wage change is a dynamic one and the reactions to the initial changes may themselves significantly affect the type and character of the results.

A new study by Levitan and Belous offers a vigorous critique of past studies of the employment effects of minimum wage changes, and an equally vigorous case for the use of minimum wage legislation to mitigate or reduce poverty among the working poor.[12]

Levitan and Belous argue, in general, that both industry and econometric studies of the employment effects of minimum wage increases under the Fair Labor Standards Act (see section immediately below) have serious limitations. While they do not contend that such increases have caused no unemployment, they minimize their impact on the job market, including the market for teenagers and other types of inexperienced or unskilled workers. They do not believe, however, that the relation of the legal minimum wage to the average wage can rise much above the ratio at which historically it has hovered without the danger of severe adverse employment consequences. But within this limitation, they hold that the income effect will tend to outweigh the employment effect, will aid in the reduction of poverty, and, in a welfare state, contribute to making work a more desirable alternative than dependence.

Some Research on Minimum Wage Employment Effects

There has been a considerable body of empirical research on the employment effects of federal minimum wage legislation. As in the case of union wage effects, as observed in the preceding chapter, this research first focused on experience in selected industries, but more recently has shifted to econometric studies relating to particular categories of workers. A major problem, of course, has been to isolate the minimum wage impact from other factors affecting employment in the industries or categories of workers concerned. It is not possible here to undertake a comprehensive review of these studies, but notice should be given to some of the more significant research findings.

Perhaps the most detailed effort to measure the economic effects on low-wage industries of an increase in the federal minimum wage was undertaken with respect to the increase from $0.75 to $1.00 an hour, which became effective March 1, 1956. Part of this program included detailed surveys by the Bureau of Labor Statistics in 12 manufacturing industries, or segments of industries, that were known to have experienced sizable payroll increases.[13] Data were collected by personal visits of bureau representatives to probability samples of establishments in each industry for single payroll periods prior to, immediately after, and typically a year after the effective date of the higher minimum. The information collected included wage rates or straight-time hourly earnings for all individual nonsupervisory workers and separately for workers in selected occupations, employee benefit practices, and general information on the ways in which employers adjusted to the higher minimum.

Briefly, the increase in the minimum wage from $0.75 to $1.00 an hour sharply increased wage levels in the low-wage industries studied. These increases ranged from 5.3 to 21.7 percent between the periods prior to and immediately after the effective date of the higher minimum. There was severe compression of the wage structures of these heavily affected industries, indicating that, at least in the short run, interpersonal and occupational differentials were not maintained. Data reflecting wage changes that occurred during the year following the initial adjustment to the higher minimum show that some restoration of differentials had taken place.

The initial decline in job differentials is not surprising, and reflects the fact that a rise in the legal minimum wage does not alter the underlying market situation for the types of labor employed by an industry. Except for considerations of morale, there is no evident immediate need for firms to grant increases to workers in higher skill classifications, especially to those whose wages already are some distance above the minimum.

A different situation presents itself where employees in essentially similar work, but differing considerably in personal efficiency, earn various amounts below the new minimum. A situation of this nature might readily result, for example, where workers in an occupation are paid on an incentive basis, or where rates are fixed on a personal rather than a job basis. If the wages of these workers of varying efficiency are raised to a uniform level (i.e., to the new minimum), the old structure of efficiency wages is destroyed. The elimination of these personal differentials through the compression of the lower end of the wage scale sets counteracting forces in motion. It is among the less efficient workers in this group that discharges are most likely to occur. Hiring standards will tend to be raised, and technical innovations affecting the relatively unskilled areas of work will tend, where feasible, to be introduced. Assuming no increase in product demand, such measures provide a basis for some curtailment of employment. These and other forces will tend over a number of years to restore wage distributions to more "normal" proportions.

The employment effects of the $1.00 minimum can be analyzed with much less assurance than the wage effects. This is partly because the data in the surveys under review did not provide a continuous record of employment. It is difficult, in any case, to disentangle the wage factor from other factors affecting the level of employment in the industries concerned. Although the period covered by the survey program was one of generally buoyant economic activity, the forces affecting product demand in particular industries were far from uniform.

Nevertheless, the rise in the minimum wage clearly produced employment effects in the industries studied. A crude indication is that employment in all except one of the 12 manufacturing industries declined between the period preceding and immediately after the effective date of the higher minimum rate. Perhaps more significantly, employment one year after the effective date was lower than in the pre-$1.00 period in all except two of the industries, the declines ranging from 3.2 percent to more than 15 percent. Nominal employment increases were registered in two industries. When the plants in the industries studied were classified by degree of impact of the minimum wage, there was a distinct tendency for employment to decline more or to increase less in those plants where the impact was "high" than where it was "low."

In the twelve industries surveyed, inquiries were made with respect to the nature of plant adjustments to the increased payroll costs associated with the higher minimum.[14] The answers provide qualitative rather than statistical insight into employment effects. As one would expect, the adjustments were various, and frequently more than one type was utilized by the same firm. They included the discharge of workers, failure to replace workers, greater care in the selection of workers, a rise in production standards, the more efficient arrangement of production sequences, increased investment in machinery and equipment, and product price increases.

The findings of the survey program on the effects of the $1.00 minimum, presented here in severely summary terms, are not atypical of the results of other studies of minimum wage impact on low-wage industries in the United States. In fact, they conform reasonably well with the findings of Tawney in his pioneering studies of initial minimum wage determinations under the British Trade Boards (Minimum Wage) Act of 1909.[15]

The industry studies show, in general, that the imposition of a minimum wage or its increase does have some employment effects in low-wage industries. They provide some indication of the kinds of adjustments employers make to the higher payroll costs involved. The employment effects may be masked, at least partially, because the timing of industry surveys may not cover the full period required for readjustment, because account cannot be taken of employment shifts to noncovered sectors or of withdrawal from the labor force, or because of expansion in product markets. Most federal minimum wage increases, in fact, have been introduced in periods of rising economic activity.

The more recent studies of the employment effects of minimum wage actions have sought to measure their impact on demographic groups, notably on teenagers.[16] The particular interest in teenagers stems from the increase in their unemployment rate during the postwar period, and the attribution of this increase by some analysts solely or largely to the statutory minimum wage.[17]

The increase in the teenage unemployment rate is incontestable. For those 16 to 19 years of age in the labor force, the unemployment rate average 10.3 percent during the 5-year period 1948–52; the average was 17.8 percent for the years 1974–78. The average rate for white teenagers increased from 10.0 percent to 15.6 percent, and for nonwhite, mainly black, teenagers from 13.0 percent to 36.3 percent. Obviously the white-black teenager unemployment ratio increased very substantially, from 1:1.3 in 1948–52 to 1:2.3 in 1974–78.

The efforts that have been made through regression analysis to measure the effects of the federal minimum wage on teenage employment have produced mixed results. A careful study by Kaitz, using

125

quarterly data for 1954–68 and annual data for the longer period 1948–68, concludes that "any measure of the effects of minimum wage laws upon teenage employment or unemployment is highly sensitive to the variables included in the analysis, the measure of minimum wage used, and the specification of the equation."[18] He adds, however, that "it should not be concluded that minimum wage laws have no effect. Rather, the fact is that time series analysis does not permit an adequate separation of various, nominally independent, factors affecting teenage employment problems." Kaitz advances as highly tentative conclusions that during the 1960s extensions of minimum wage coverage had more effect on changes in the teenage unemployment rate than increases in the minimum wage; that federal manpower programs have tended to offset decreases in teenage employment attributed to the minimum; and that there is some evidence to support the hypothesis that minimum wages have had greater adverse effects upon 16 to 17 year olds than upon 18 to 19 year olds.

Other econometric studies point to measurable minimum wage effects on the employment of teenagers. Kosters and Welch, for example, conclude that "increases in the effective minimum wage over the period 1954–68 have had a significant impact on employment patterns. Minimum wage legislation has had the effect of decreasing the share of normal employment and increasing vulnerability to cyclical changes in employment for the groups most 'marginal' to the work force—teenagers. Thus as a result of increased minimum wages, teenagers are able to obtain fewer jobs during periods of normal employment growth and their jobs are less secure in the face of short-term employment changes."[19]

In a particularly interesting study, Mincer emphasizes the employment and labor force, rather than the unemployment, effects of minimum wage legislation.[20] His empirical analysis, which relates to the period 1954–69, indicates that, as a consequence of minimum wage increases, labor moves out of the covered sector into the uncovered sector and out of the labor market. Wages in the uncovered sector fall. No more than a third of the employment loss in the covered sector appears as unemployment, the bulk of the remainder representing withdrawal from the labor force. This withdrawal probably is facilitated by the availability of alternatives, such as retirement, welfare, and school enrollment. The largest *disemployment* effects

126

were observed for nonwhite teenagers, followed by nonwhite males (20–24), white teenagers, and white males (20–24). The largest increases in unemployment were experienced by the same groups, although not in the same order.

A broad-gauged study by Gramlich seeks to throw light on the effects of minimum wage actions on family income distribution as well as on employment.[21] The details of his analysis, which deserve careful attention, do not lend themselves to a brief summary. With respect to income distribution, his general conclusion, advanced somewhat tentatively, is "that as long as minimum wages are kept low relative to other wages, they are not terribly harmful and in fact even have slightly beneficial effects both on low-wage workers and on the overall distribution of income."[22] To minimize adverse employment and other effects, the minimum wage, in his view, should not be increased beyond its historical relationship with the median wage (in the range of 40 to 50 percent). And he casts a "moderately strong vote" for a differential in the minimum for teenagers, with monitoring of the extent to which a lower rate for teenagers results in their substitution for adults in employment.

Episodic increases in the uniform minimum wage standard have been, on the whole, a relatively minor factor in the *general* upward movement of money wages in the United States. However, the broad extensions of coverage beginning in the early 1960s enhanced the economic significance of minimum wage actions, and the 1977 amendments to the Fair Labor Standards Act provided, in essence, for annual escalation of the minimum rate for the period 1978–81.

On some demographic groups, geographic areas, and industries, the impact of minimum wage changes has been comparatively heavy. The employment effects of these changes, as indicated above, are difficult to measure with any precision. They may be partially obscured by transfers to uncovered employment, withdrawals from the labor force, government job creation, and expansion in economic activity. The rise in teenage unemployment, which has received so much attention in recent years, surely has a complex of causes. But minimum wage increase, although the evidence is not unambiguous, would appear to be a contributing factor of some significance.

Evidence on employment effects does not destroy the case for well-devised minimum wage action. There are other considerations, as emphasized by Levitan and Belous, that cannot be explored here. But

127

clearly minimum wage determinations should be made with great care to limit adverse employment effects on marginal components of the labor force. Their impact on teenage employment would appear to need particular attention. A youth differential, opposed by organized labor and rejected on several occasions by the Congress, is one measure that may warrant additional consideration.

Suggested Readings

Much insight into the present state of the long controversy over the income and employment effects of legal minimum wage determinations can be gained from Sar A. Levitan and Richard S. Belous' *More Than Subsistence: Minimum Wages for the Working Poor* (Baltimore: Johns Hopkins University Press, 1979), and from Finis Welch's *Minimum Wages: Issues and Evidence* (Washington, D.C.: American Enterprise Institute, 1978). See also Edward M. Gramlich's "Impact of Minimum Wages on Other Wages, Employment, and Family Incomes," *Brookings Papers on Economic Activity*, 2, 1976, and Jacob Mincer, "Unemployment Effects of Minimum Wages," *Journal of Political Economy*, part 2, August 1976. Bulletin 1657 of the U.S. Bureau of Labor Statistics, *Youth Unemployment and Minimum Wages* (Washington, D.C.: GPO, 1970), deals with various aspects of the question, including foreign experience with wage differentials for young workers.

11

Concluding Observations

The level of employment—or the level and composition of unemployment—has been a major concern of economic policy during the period since World War II. There clearly is an intimate relationship between employment and the structure of wages and the dynamics of wage change.

An attempt has been made in this small monograph to outline some of the major aspects of our wage experience. There is historical continuity in that experience, in the sense that we have relied primarily on the operation of demand-supply forces in the labor market to shape the structure of wages and to determine the magnitude of change in the general level of compensation.

If there is a partial dichotomy in this experience, its roots are found in the social and ideologicl changes that began to take shape during the great depression of the 1930s. These were strengthened and extended during the years following World War II. Although the labor market remains the primary mechanism through which wages are determined, these changes have, in some measure and in various ways, affected its operation.

The major changes that mark the postwar period include, most importantly, the revolution in economic thought by Keynes and his interpreters, in particular the role assigned to fiscal and monetary policy in maintaining high levels of output and employment.[1] This was accompanied by the political acceptance of full employment (however defined) as a major goal of public policy, as reflected in the passage of the Employment Act of 1946. But federal policy has consisted not only of measures to influence the general operation of the economy, but has sought increasingly since the mid-1930s to achieve particular economic and social objectives.

Many of the particular government policies and programs have some direct relevance for the functioning of the labor market. These include the rise of social insurance systems to provide income protection against unemployment and old-age dependency; the great growth during the postwar period of provisions for welfare assistance; the creation through law of a clear national labor policy guaranteeing to workers the right to organize and imposing upon employers the duty to bargain over wages and other conditions of employment; the proliferation of federal manpower training and employment programs from modest beginnings in the early 1960s; the effort, given legislative content in 1964, to end discrimination in employment against blacks, other minority groups, and women; the establishment, periodic increase, and extension of coverage of a national minimum wage; the encouragement, through guaranteed student loans and in other ways, of access to higher education; and the several efforts, following the war-induced wage stabilization program, to restrain the rate of wage increase through voluntary or mandatory wage control programs.

These developments, considered together, created a labor market framework that differed considerably from that which had existed throughout the nineteenth and indeed the first third of the twentieth century. Their labor market consequences were various. Social security (and the rise of private pension plans) facilitated the withdrawal of older workers from the labor market. Unemployment insurance, certainly for some workers, made feasible more extended periods of job search, and, aside from this effect, may have had at least a marginal influence on the unemployment rate. A side effect of the large growth of a government-financed welfare system probably has been to raise the reserve price of labor and has provided, for some, an alternative to work.

Investment in "human capital" through education and training has been enhanced through federal programs in these areas, and has facilitated labor force adjustment to the many changes in postwar occupational requirements in the American economy. The effort to end discrimination in employment has opened new job opportunities for minorities and women, and new sources of supply to many jobs, but has created also some problems of personnel administration.

The establishment of trade unionism as a stable labor market institution in many sectors of the economy has served to dilute competition in the labor market, and has provided workers with a vehicle for the expression of their preferences in the wage bargain. The legal minimum wage, with its extensive but not universal coverage, serves as an anchor to the wage structure. Finally, the episodic efforts of the federal government to influence the rate of wage increase represent interventions into the operation of the labor market not found in any earlier period. They reflect a response to new factors in the postwar situation, particularly the government's commitment to the maintenance of high level employment, the market power associated with the spread of trade unionism, and concern with wages as a source of pressure on prices from the side of cost.

Alterations in the labor market framework came not only from the side of government. There has been a growth of professionalism in wage administration, flowing partially from wartime experience and, as the postwar period developed, from the increasing complexity of the wage bargain. Expectations of regularity in gains in money and real wages became, in a sense, partially institutionalized among workers. As the postwar period lengthened, attitudes toward jobs and work seemed to undergo change, particularly among the increasing segment of the labor force that had experienced only relatively high levels of employment.

It was within this somewhat altered framework that the labor market had to cope during the postwar period with two major developments on the supply side: a greatly enlarged influx of young people, beginning about the mid-1960s; and a sharp increase in the participation rate of women in the labor force. The total civilian labor force grew by about 41 million, or by 69 percent, between 1947 and 1978. This large increase in supply accomodated, and perhaps in a measure was a response to, expansion in the demand for labor in an economy that, with some interruptions, grew strongly in real terms. The postwar era also witnessed great changes in the occupational composition of the labor force, with the direction in terms of rates of increase toward white-collar as against manual employments.

The deployment in jobs throughout the economy of this great labor force expansion was accomplished largely through the labor market. A broad view of the wage structure that resulted from the play of market forces, including the institutional and social constraints under which the market operates, was presented in Chapter 4. This structure evidently was sufficient to induce the education, training, and labor mobility necessary to meet postwar occupational requirements.

The fact must be emphasized that the structure of wages and salaries in the United States is highly complex. Its broad contours can be defined and described. But within these contours there are numerous sources of variation. This is suggested by the comparatively wide dispersion of rates of pay within occupations. The relative dispersion of pay appears greatest for relatively unskilled manual jobs and lowest for professional and administrative occupations.

Wage rate dispersion is in some measure a reflection of the efficiency with which the labor market operates, but other factors, including collective bargaining status and industry location, also play a part. Dispersion also arises from differences in the quality or productiveness of workers within an occupation. Such differences tend roughly to be taken into account through methods of wage payment and the personnel selection process.

One of the striking developments in the United States, and not in the United States alone, has been the tendency for occupational pay differentials to decline during the twentieth century. This tendency has been best documented in the case of the differential for skilled as against unskilled manual work, but it appears to have a much broader incidence. This result has flowed basically from the operation of supply-demand forces in the labor market, with perhaps a marginal effect from legal minimum wage determinations and other government wage actions, and, in some situations, from trade union wage policy. Inflation seems to serve as a special factor in the contraction of pay differentials, as seen most clearly in the operation of formal cost-of-living escalator arrangements, where adjustments almost invariably are made in uniform cents-per-hour terms.

Although social policy may favor still greater reduction in occupational pay differences, arbitrary efforts to reduce wage differentials through government action would raise all of the formidable problems of price control. The longer-range approach is to enhance the supply of workers to those occupations that command relatively high pay. By and large, the great increase in opportunities for education and training in the United States works in this direction. Undoubtedly a major difficulty, as Phelps Brown emphasizes in his detailed analysis of the question of pay inequality, is somehow to break through the barriers to learning and achievement often encountered in the home by children in low-income and poorly educated families.[2]

Since 1938, the federal government has played a direct role in the wage-setting process through legal minimum wage actions. This has been a limited role; it has been exercised, on the whole, with considerable regard for its possible adverse employment effects. There inevitably have been such effects, however, as employers in low-wage industries and areas have sought in various ways to offset the higher labor costs involved. There also have been favorable income effects, and it is difficult to judge the extent to which the two types of effects have balanced out. In recent years, great interest has centered on minimum wage actions in relation to the rising rate of teenage unemployment. Certainly demographic and other factors have contributed importantly to this development. But especially with the extension of coverage to many traditional sources of employment for relatively large numbers of young people, additional consideration probably should be given to a lower legal minimum rate for young and inexperienced workers.

The postwar efforts to restrain generally the rate of increase in wages (and prices) represents a second type of federal intervention in the wage determination process. Such "income policies" reflect, on the wage side, the spread of collective bargaining, and an effort to dampen union market power under conditions of high level employment. They are essentially efforts to control inflation from the cost side. Experience in this and other industrial countries suggests that their role is at best secondary, for inflation sets in motion forces that tend to affect rates of increase in wages generally and not in the unionized sector alone. The convergence of a price-wage or a wage-price spiral appears to depend much more on the rigid application of other disinflationary measures. At the same time, bringing an inflationary episode under control may well be made more difficult if such devices as cost-of-living escalator clauses become deeply imbedded in the wage-setting process, especially if the effort is to achieve gains in real wages that are, in the circumstances, unsustainable. Here the element of expectations with respect to regularity of increase in money and real wages, which tended to develop during the postwar period, comes into play.

Despite its comparative ineffectiveness thus far, social concern with general "wage policy" probably will continue to exist, given the government commitment to high level employment and to various direct labor market programs. The essential problem actually is to avoid the creation of inflationary pressures through fiscal and monetary policy, and to restrain, through a variety of strategies, the exercise of market power by unions or employers; that is, from the side of either wages or administered prices. This emphatically is not to say that unions should cease to function as an important labor market institution, for they provide workers through the collective bargaining process with a voice in the determination of wages and other conditions of work that can be obtained in no other way. But attention needs to be given to the employment effects of wage bargains on the allocation of workers among employments and on costs, prices, and employment generally. It will be recalled in this connection that the evidence seems to indicate that the market power of unions tends to be exaggerated.

The review of the historical wage experience of American workers showed that real wages, with some pauses and interruptions, advanced during the nineteenth century largely through the operation of a highly competitive labor market. This result was achieved, taking the century as a whole, through rising money rates of pay coupled with a generally declining level of consumer prices. It was underpinned, of course, by the advancing productivity of American industry and agriculture. The gain in real wages continued during the first part of the twentieth century, despite two world wars and a devastating depression. In fact, the average annual rage of increase in real wages during the years 1900–47 appears to have exceeded the nineteenth century rate. During this period, money wages rose sharply, more than matching the steep rise in consumer prices associated with the two wars. Trade unionism after 1900 became a more important factor in the operation of the labor market.

During the post-World War II period, the average annual rate of increase in real wages was much greater during the years to 1966 than subsequently. Beginning about 1966, two major problems arose: an inflationary movement that now (1979) represents the longest such episode in American history; and a marked decline in the rate of productivity increase. Both of these developments cloud the outlook for future advance in real rates of pay and have implications for employment as well.

In an economy as complex as that of the United States, primary reliance in wage determination will continue to revolve about the labor market, with market impulses filtered through the collective bargaining process in important areas of employment. Clearly the market will function more effectively the better it is organized. This means continued growth in information on the current and prospective demand for and supply of various types of workers; educational and training facilities that are sensitive to labor market developments; and the strengthening of employment placement services. Competition in the labor market (among employers for workers and workers for jobs) will tend to produce a structure of wage differentials appropriate at a particular time, given production functions and the character of consumer demand for goods and services.

It is important in terms of employment that the wage system have sufficient flexibility to accomodate, at least in a rough way, the differences in quality or productivity that exist among workers in the same grade or occupation. This can be accomplished through the use of wage payment methods that yield variable rates (rate ranges, incentive systems) or through the personnel selection process among firms with different wage levels. It is important also that the systems of income support payments that have developed since the 1930s, notably unemployment insurance and public welfare, should not, on any appreciable scale, provide alternatives to work for those who are otherwise capable of gainful employment.

Notes

Chapter 1

1. A useful account of the various measures of wage rates, earnings, and employee compensation currently prepared by the U.S. Bureau of Labor Statistics will be found in its Bulletin 1941, *BLS Measures of Compensation* (Washington, D.C.: GPO, 1977).

Chapter 2

1. Earned rates are computed by dividing earnings for a given payroll period by hours worked or paid for.

2. See U.S. Department of Labor, Bureau of Labor Statistics, Bulletin 1425–15, *Hours, Overtime, and Weekend Work* (Washington, D.C.: GPO, 1974).

3. U.S. Department of Labor, Bureau of Labor Statistics, Bulletin 1948, *Industry Wage Survey: Petroleum Refining, April 1976* (Washington, D.C.: GPO, 1977), p. 4, and table 17, p. 23.

4. U.S. Department of Labor, Bureau of Labor Statistics, Bulletin 1952, *Industry Wage Survey: Nonferrous Foundries, May 1975* (Washington, D.C.: GPO, 1977), table 23, p. 27.

5. U.S. Department of Labor, *The Termination Report of the National War Labor Board* (Washington, D.C.: GPO, 1948), 1, pp. 306–403.

6. Voluntary (in contrast to dispute) cases were those presented jointly by unions and employers, or, in the absence of unions, by employers alone. The great bulk of the cases were of this nature.

7. U.S. Department of Labor, Bureau of Labor Statistics, Bulletin 1850–89, *Area Wage Surveys: Metropolitan Areas, United States and Regional Summaries, 1975* (Washington, D.C.: GPO, 1977), pp. 94–99.

8. Ibid., table 12, p. 100.

9. Albert Rees, *New Measures of Wage-Earner Compensation in Manufacturing, 1914–1957* (New York: National Bureau of Economic Research, Occasional Paper 75, 1960), table 1, pp. 3–4.

10. U.S. Department of Labor, Bureau of Labor Statistics; Bulletin 1963, *Employee Compensation in the Private Nonfarm Economy* (Washington, D.C.: GPO, 1977), table 23, p. 36.

11. William V. Deutermann, Jr., and Scott Campbell Brown, "Voluntary Part-Time Workers: A Growing Part of the Labor Force," *Monthly Labor Review,* June 1978, table 1, p. 5.

12. See Martin Feldstein, "The Unemployment Caused by Unemployment Insurance," and Ronald L. Oaxaca, "Impacts of Unemployment Insurance on the Duration of Unemployment and the Post-Unemployment Wage," *Proceedings,* 28th Annual Winter Meeting, Industrial Relations Research Association, 1975, pp. 225–33 and 234–41.

13. For a brief account of the Consumer Price Index and its most recent revision, see the following U.S. Bureau of Labor Statistics publications: *The Consumer Price Index: Concepts and Content Over the Years* (1978) and *Revising the Consumer Price Index* (1978).

14. For a description of the concepts, procedures, and uses of standard budgets, see U.S. Department of Labor, Bureau of Labor Statistics, Bulletin 1570–75, *Three Standards of Living for an Urban Family of Four Persons* (Washington, D.C.: GPO, 1969). For the most recent pricing of these budgets, see U.S. Department of Labor press release 79–305 (April 29, 1979), "Autumn 1978 Urban Family Budgets and Comparative Indexes for Selected Urban Areas."

Chapter 3

1. Beverly L. Johnson, "Changes in Marital and Family Characteristics of Workers, 1970–78," *Monthly Labor Review,* April 1979, pp. 49–52.

2. E. H. Phelps Brown, *The Economics of Labor* (New Haven, Conn.: Yale University Press, 1962), chap. 5.

3. Adam Smith, *The Wealth of Nations* (Oxford: Oxford University Press, World Classics edition), 1, p. 83.

4. Allan Flanders, "Collective Bargaining: A Theoretical Analysis," *British Journal of Industrial Relations,* March 1968, p. 26.

5. See Craufurd D. Goodwin (editor), *Exhortation and Controls: The Search for a Wage-Price Policy, 1945–1971* (Washington, D.C.: Brookings Institution, 1975).

6. National Commission on Employment and Unemployment Statistics, *Counting the Labor Force* (Washington, D.C.: GPO, 1979). Detailed labor force data will be found each month in *Employment and Earnings,* issued by the U.S. Bureau of Labor Statistics.

7. The U.S. Bureau of Labor Statistics prepares an extensive *Occupational Outlook Handbook* on a biennial basis. The most recent edition is for 1978–79.

8. Stanley Lebergott, *Manpower in Economic Growth: The American Record Since 1800* (New York: McGraw-Hill, 1964), p. 155.

9. U.S. Department of Labor, Bureau of Labor Statistics, Bulletin 2020, *Occupational Projections and Training Data* (Washington, D.C.: GPO, 1979), p. 19. See also A. J. Jaffe and Joseph Froomkin, "Occupational Opportunities for College-educated Workers, 1950–75," *Monthly Labor Review,* June 1978, pp. 15–21.

Chapter 4

1. Samuel Saben, "Occupational Mobility of Employed Workers," *Monthly Labor Review,* June 1967, pp. 31–38.

2. U.S. Department of Labor, Manpower Administration, *Dictionary of Occupational Titles* (Washington, D.C.: GPO, 1965). Various supplements to the third edition have been issued.

3. International Labor Office, *International Standard Classification of Occupations* (Geneva, Switzerland, 1969).

4. There is a fairly extensive literature on job evaluation, in part directed to specific applications (e.g., metalworking establishments, offices).

5. U.S. Department of Labor, Bureau of Labor Statistics, Supplement (1974–77) to Bulletin 1814, *Wage Chronology: United States Steel Corporation and United Steelworkers of America* (Washington, D.C., 1975), p. 6.

6. U.S. Department of Labor, Bureau of Labor Statistics, Bulletin 1893, *Wage Chronology: Rockwell International (Electronics, North American Aircraft/Space Operations) and UAW, May 1941–September 1977* (Washington, D.C.: GPO, 1976), p. 35.

7. U.S. Department of Labor, Bureau of Labor Statistics, Bulletin 1904, *Wage Chronology: Lockheed-California Company (Division of Lockheed Aircraft Corporation) and Machinists' Union, March 1937–October 1977* (Washington, D.C.: GPO, 1976). p. 31.

Chapter 5

1. Harry Ober, "Occupational Wage Differentials, 1907–1947," *Monthly Labor Review,* August 1948, pp. 127–34.

2. The estimates beginning with 1953 represent the unweighted averages of the median wage relationships of individual skilled occupations to the rates for male janitors within establishments. Prior to 1953, the estimates were based on group averages for unskilled and skilled work.

3. U.S. Department of Labor, Bureau of Labor Statistics, Bulletin 1575–87, *Wages and Related Benefits, Part II: Metropolitan Areas, United States and Regional Summaries, 1967–68* (Washington, D.C.: GPO, 1969), table 10, pp. 90–91.

4. Melvin W. Reder, "The Theory of Occupational Wage Differentials," *American Economic Review,* December 1955, pp. 833–52.

5. Ibid., p. 838.

6. There is little information on the form of wage increases during World War I, and information on wage movements generally is not abundant. A useful work for the period to the end of 1917 is Hugh S. Hanna and W. Jett Lauck, *Wages and the War: A Summary of Recent Wage Movements* (Cleveland, Ohio: Doyle and Waltz Printing Co., 1918). See also U.S. Department of Labor, Bureau of Labor Statistics, Bulletin 852, *War and Postwar Wages, Prices, and Hours, 1914–23 and 1939–44* (Washington, D.C.: GPO, 1946).

7. H. M. Douty, "Union Impact on Wage Structures," *Proceedings,* Sixth Annual Winter Meeting, Industrial Relations Research Association, 1953, pp. 61–76.

8. H. M. Douty, "Wage Policy and the Role of Fact-Finding Boards," *Monthly Labor Review,* April 1946, pp. 537–49.

9. By the early 1950s, a vast majority of the plant workers in manufacturing were in establishments with formal single or rate-range structures. See Otto Hollberg, "Wage Formalization in Major Labor Markets, 1951–52," *Monthly Labor Review,* January 1953, pp. 22–26.

10. Arnold R. Weber and Daniel J. B. Mitchell, *The Pay Board's Progress: Wage Controls in Phase II* (Washington, D.C.: Brookings Institution, 1978), p. 57.

11. Ibid., pp. 127–35.

12. John Stuart Mill, *Principles of Political Economy,* Ashley edition (London: Longmans, Green and Co.), p. 392.

13. U.S. Department of Labor, Bureau of Labor Statistics, Bulletin 1865, *Handbook of Labor Statistics, 1975* (Washington, D.C.: GPO, 1975), table 108, pp. 266–74. This index was discontinued in 1973.

14. Tibor Scitovsky, "An International Comparison of the Trend of Professional Earnings," *American Economic Review,* March 1966, pp. 25–42.

15. Ibid., p. 26.

16. Ibid., pp. 31–32.

17. Changes in public school teacher salaries were calculated from Edward J. Wasilewski, "Teachers' Salaries for the 1977–78 School Year," *Current Wage Developments,* March 1979, table 2, p. 39; for production and nonsupervisory workers in the private nonfarm economy, the Bureau of Labor Statistics Hourly Earnings Index, published regularly in *Current Wage Developments,* provides an approximation of wage rate change.

18. Between 1925 and 1978, the average salaries of public school teachers increased by almost 700 percent; the increase in the average hourly earnings of production and related workers in manufacturing was more than 1,000 percent. For teachers, ibid.; for manufacturing workers, Bureau of Labor Statistics, *Handbook of Labor Statistics, 1975,* table 98, p. 248, and *Monthly Labor Review,* April 1979, table 14, p. 85.

19. H. M. Douty, " 'Fair Comparison': The Case of the United States White-Collar Civil Service," *Economica,* November 1965, pp. 375–92.

20. Henry Phelps Brown, *The Inequality of Pay* (Berkeley and Los Angeles: University of California Press, 1977), p. 99.

Chapter 6

1. First Annual Report of the Commissioner of Labor, *Industrial Depressions* (Washington, D.C.: GPO, 1886), p. 142.

2. Charles Booth, *Life and Labour of the People in London,* Second Series, V (London: Macmillan, 1903), p. 203.

3. Lloyd G. Reynolds, "Wage Differences in Local Labor Markets," *American Economic Review,* June 1946, p. 366.

4. N. Arnold Tolles and Robert L. Raimon, *Sources of Wage Information: Employer Associations* (Ithaca, N.Y.: Cornell University Press, 1952), p. 240.

5. Alfred Marshall, *Principles of Economics,* 8th ed. (London: Macmillan, 1920), p. 547.

6. See Robert Evans, Jr., "Worker Quality and Wage Dispersion: An Analysis of a Clerical Labor Market in Boston," *Proceedings,* 14th Annual Winter Meeting, Industrial Relations Research Association, 1961, pp. 246–59.

7. H. M. Douty, "Some Aspects of Wage Statistics and Wage Theory," *Proceedings,* 11th Annual Winter Meeting, Industrial Relations Research Association, 1958, pp. 196–211.

8. Jerome A. Mark, "Measurement of Job Performance and Age," *Monthly Labor Review,* December 1956, pp. 1410–14.

9. U.S. Department of Labor, Bureau of Labor Statistics, Bulletin 1345–83, *Wages and Related Benefits,* part 2: *Metropolitan Areas, United States and Regional Summaries, 1962–63* (Washington, D.C.: GPO, 1964), pp. 61–64.

10. U.S. Department of Labor, Bureau of Labor Statistics, Bulletin 1425–17, *Major Collective Bargaining Agreements: Wage Administration Provisions* (Washington, D.C.: GPO, 1978), p. 1.

11. Ibid., pp. 2–13; table 1, p. 45; and table 2, p. 46.

12. Walter A. Fogel, "Job Rate Ranges: A Theoretical and Empirical Analysis," *Industrial and Labor Relations Review,* July 1964, pp. 584–97.

13. George P. Shultz, Irwin L. Herrnstadt, and Elbridge S. Puckett, "Wage Determination in a Non-Union Labor Market," *Proceedings,* 10th Annual Winter Meeting, Industrial Relations Research Association, 1957, p. 204.

14. H. M. Douty, "Sources of Occupational Wage and Salary Rate Dispersion within Labor Markets," *Industrial and Labor Relations Review,* October 1961, pp. 67–74.

15. Albert Rees and George P. Shultz, *Workers and Wages in an Urban Labor Market* (Chicago: University of Chicago Press, 1970).

16. Ibid., p. 222.

Chapter 7

1. For 1800–1974: Bureau of Labor Statistics *Handbook of Labor Statistics 1975,* table 122, p. 313; for 1975–78, *Monthly Labor Review,* April 1979, table 22, p. 93.

2. John W. Kendrick, *Understanding Productivity* (Baltimore: Johns Hopkins University Press, 1977).

3. Adam Smith, *The Wealth of Nations* (Oxford University Press, World's Classics edition), vol. 1, book 1, chap. 8, p. 77.

4. Ibid.

5. Ibid., vol. 2, bk. 4, chap. 7, pp. 162–63.

6. Paul A. David, "The Growth of Real Product in the United States before 1840: New Evidence, Controlled Conjectures," *Journal of Economic History,* June 1967, pp. 151–97.

7. Robert E. Gallman, "Commodity Output, 1839–1899," in National Bureau of Economic Research, *Trends in the American Economy in the Nineteenth Century,* Studies in Income and Wealth, Vol. 24 (Princeton, N.J.: Princeton University Press, 1960), table 1, p. 16.

8. Sir S. Morton Peto, *Resources and Prospects of America* (New York: Alexander Strahan and Co., 1866), p. 94.

9. J. Frederic Dewhurst and Associates, *America's Needs and Resources* (New York: Twentieth Century Fund, 1955), table 14, p. 40.

10. Gallman, *op. cit.,* table 1, p. 16.

11. U.S. Department of Commerce, Bureau of the Census, *Historical Statistics of the United States: Colonial Times to 1957* (Washington, D.C.: GPO, 1960), series W-1, p. 599.

12. The "private business sector" excludes government and the output of private households and nonprofit institutions. See J. R. Norsworthy and L. J. Fulco, "New Sector Definitions for Productivity Series," *Monthly Labor Review,* October 1976, pp. 40–42.

13. Stanley Lebergott, *Manpower in Economic Growth: The American Record Since 1800* (New York: McGraw-Hill, 1964), especially chaps. 6 and 7 and appendix tables A-20 to A-29.

14. Some support for this conclusion is given by the behavior of wages in Philadelphia. See Donald R. Adams, Jr., "Wage Rates in the Early National Period:

Philadelphia, 1785–1830," *Journal of Economic History,* September 1968, pp. 404–26.

15. U.S. Senate Committee on Finance, Report by Mr. Aldrich, *Wholesale Prices, Wages, and Transportation* (Washington, D.C.: GPO, 1893). The wage data are shown in detail in table 12 beginning on p. 293 of part 2, extending through part 3, and ending on p. 1560 of part 4.

16. Ibid., part 1, p. 176.

17. Ibid., part 4, table 13, pp. 1561–72.

18. Ibid., part 4, table 14, pp. 1573–81.

19. Lebergott, op. cit., appendix table A-32. The derivation of the index is explained on pp. 334–37.

20. See testimony of Ethel D. Hoover at Hearings, Joint Economic Committee, 86th Congress, 1st session, on *Employment, Growth, and Price Levels,* part 2, pp. 384ff.

21. Lebergott, op. cit., p. 154.

22. Lebergott, op. cit., table A-1, p. 510.

23. Clarence D. Long, *Wages and Earnings in the United States, 1860–90* (Princeton, N.J.: Princeton University Press, 1960), table A-1, pp. 121–24. Average wages were shown by Long for January and July of each year. For the computation of annual index numbers, these averages have been combined.

24. Albert Rees, *Real Wages in Manufacturing, 1890–1914* (Princeton, N.J.: Princeton University Press, 1961), table 10, p. 33.

25. Lebergott, op. cit., pp. 289–95.

26. Lebergott also presents a series on average daily wages for "nonfarm employees" for 1860–80, but the movement of that series is practically identical with that of his annual earnings series for those years. See ibid., pp. 295–304 and table A-19, p. 528.

27. Rees, op. cit., table 43, p. 117. For Mrs. Hoover's index, see note 20, above. Lebergott prepared a cost of living index for 1860–80 which differs in its behavior from the Hoover index used here. See Lebergott, op. cit., pp. 337–52, and table A-33, p. 549.

28. Long, op. cit., p. 115.

29. Lebergott, op. cit., table A-1, p. 510.

30. Leo Wolman, *Ebb and Flow in Trade Unionism* (New York: National Bureau of Economic Research, 1936), table 5, p. 16.

31. Robert Ozanne, *Wages in Practice and Theory: McCormick and International Harvester, 1860–1960* (Madison, Wis.: University of Wisconsin Press, 1968).

32. See Alvin H. Hansen, *Monetary Theory and Fiscal Policy* (New York: McGraw-Hill, 1949), pp. 143–55.

33. For a fascinating account of product and price changes during this period, see Dorothy S. Brady, "Relative Prices in the Nineteenth Century," *Journal of Economic History*, June 1964, pp. 145–203.

34. H. J. Habakkuk, *American and British Technology in the Nineteenth Century* (Cambridge: University of Cambridge Press, 1962).

35. Lebergott, op. cit., p. 228.

36. Wolman, op. cit., table 27, p. 116.

37. Ibid., table 19, p. 87.

38. Paul H. Douglas, *Real Wages in the United States, 1890–1926* (Boston: Houghton Mifflin Co., 1930).

39. Bureau of the Census, *Historical Statistics of the United States: Colonial Times to 1957*, series D1-12, p. 70.

40. See H. M. Douty, "The Development of Wage-Price Policies," in U. S. Bureau of Labor Statistics, Bulletin 1009, *Problems and Policies of Dispute Settlement and Wage Stabilization During World War II* (Washington, D.C.: GPO, 1950), pp. 104–54; and John T. Dunlop, "An Appraisal of Wage Stabilization Policies," ibid., pp. 155–86.

41. Computed from "Trends in Urban Wage Rates, September 1947," *Monthly Labor Review*, January 1948, table 1, p. 45.

42. *Twentieth Anniversary of the Employment Act of 1946: An Economic Symposium* (U.S. Congress, Joint Economic Committee, 89th Congress, 2d session, 1966).

43. The labor force and employment estimates are not strictly comparable for 1947 and 1978, mainly because of adjustments in certain years to census data, and, beginning in 1960, the inclusion of Alaska and Hawaii in the estimates.

44. E. J. Mishan, *The Costs of Economic Growth* (London: Staples Press, 1967). For a restatement of the "anti-growth" thesis, see Mishan's paper on "What Happened to Progress?" *Journal of Economic Issues*, June 1978, pp. 405–25.

45. Other earnings series for the post-World War II period that can be expressed in real terms include average weekly earnings, average spendable weekly earnings, and average compensation per hour. Each is appropriate for some purposes. The differences among them are discussed in a useful article by Thomas W. Gavett, "Measures of Change in Real Wages and Earnings," *Monthly Labor Review*, February 1972, pp. 48–53.

Chapter 8

1. See Joseph W. Duncan and William C. Shelton, *Revolution in U.S. Government Statistics, 1926–1976* (Washington, D.C.: GPO, 1978).

2. Nelson M. Bortz, "Cost-of-Living Clauses and the UAW-GM Pact," *Monthly Labor Review*, July 1948, pp. 1–7. See also Joseph W. Garbarino, *Wage Policy and Long-Term Contracts* (Washington, D.C.: Brookings Institution, 1962), especially chap. 2.

3. U.S. Department of Labor, Bureau of Labor Statistics, Bulletin 2013, *Characteristics of Major Collective Bargaining Agreements, July 1, 1976* (Washington, D.C.: GPO, 1979), table 1.4, p. 6.

4. Judith A. Finger, "Wage-Rate Increases in Major Agreements in 1977 Smaller than Any Year since 1973," *Current Wage Developments,* April 1978, table B, p. 47.

5. *Economic Report of the President,* 1962, pp. 185–90; see also John Sheahan, *The Wage-Price Guideposts* (Washington, D.C.: Brookings Institution, 1967).

6. E.H. Phelps Brown, "The Analysis of Wage Movements Under Full Employment," *Scottish Journal of Political Economy*, November 1971, pp. 239–40.

7. For the statistical evidence, see *Economic Report of the President*, 1972, table 8, p. 48, and table 9, p. 49.

8. Finger, loc. cit., p. 45 and table A, p. 46.

9. George H. Hildebrand, "Wage Policy and Business Activity," *Proceedings*, 11th Annual Winter Meeting, Industrial Relations Research Association, 1958, p. 176.

10. The secular rate of productivity growth indicates the extent to which the consumption of goods or services or of leisure, or of some combination of these, can be increased. How productivity gains are actually distributed as between labor and property income, or among different groups of workers within the labor force, is a function of money wage and price determination.

11. *Current Wage Developments*, September 1976, pp. 1–2.

12. *Current Wage Developments*, April 1978, table B, p. 47.

13. Douglas R. LeRoy, "Scheduled Wage Increases and Escalator Provisions in 1978," *Monthly Labor Review*, January 1978, pp. 3–8.

14. H. M. Douty, *Cost-of-Living Escalator Clauses and Inflation* (Washington, D.C.: Council on Wage and Price Stability, 1975), table 7, p. 27. A good account of the factors determining the yield of escalator clauses will be found in Victor J. Sheifer, "Cost-of-Living Adjustment: Keeping up with Inflation?" *Monthly Labor Review*, June 1979, pp. 14–17.

15. Nicholas S. Perna, "The Contractual Cost-of-Living Escalator," Federal Reserve Bank of New York, *Monthly Review*, July 1974, pp. 177–82.

16. Bureau of Labor Statistics Bulletin 2013, *Characteristics of Major Collective Bargaining Agreements, July 1, 1976,* table 3.18, p. 40.

17. *Economic Report of the President*, 1967, p. 129.

18. On the question of wage escalation and inflation in the present circumstances, see Douty, op. cit., pp. 45–55; and Daniel J. B. Mitchell, "Escalators, Inflation, and Macroeconomic Policy," *Proceedings*, 31st Annual Winter Meeting, Industrial Relations Research Association, 1978, pp. 264–70.

Chapter 9

1. Combined union and employee association membership data are available only since 1968. For the 1975 and 1976 figures, separately and in combination, see U.S. Department of Labor, release 77-771, "Labor Union and Employee Association Membership—1976"; for 1968–74, see U.S. Bureau of Labor Statistics, Bulletin 1937, *Directory of National Unions and Employee Associations, 1975* (Washington, D.C.: GPO, 1977), table 6, p. 63; for union membership only, 1930–68, see U.S. Bureau of Labor Statistics release (June 1970), "Union Membership as a Proportion of Labor Force, 1930–68."

2. H. M. Douty, "The Impact of Trade Unionism on Internal Wage Structures," in J. L. Meij (editor), *Internal Wage Structure* (Amsterdam: North-Holland Publishing Co., 1963), pp. 222–59.

3. J. Pen, *The Wage Rate under Collective Bargaining* (Cambridge, Mass.: Harvard University Press, 1959). See also G.L.S. Shackle, "The Nature of the Bargaining Process," in John T. Dunlop (editor), *The Theory of Wage Determination* (London: Macmillan, 1957), pp. 292–314, and the discussion of this paper, pp. 355–59.

4. H.G. Lewis, *Unionism and Relative Wages in the United States* (Chicago: University of Chicago Press, 1963). See also the perceptive review of Lewis' study by M. W. Reder, "Unions and Wages: The Problems of Measurement," *Journal of Political Economy*, April 1965, pp. 188–96.

5. Lewis, op. cit., table 50, p. 193.

6. Ibid., table 64, p. 222.

7. Michael J. Boskin, "Unions and Relative Real Wages," *American Economic Review,* June 1972, pp. 466–72.

8. See Orley Ashenfelter, "Discrimination and Trade Unions," in Orley Ashenfelter and Albert Rees (editors), *Discrimination in Labor Markets* (Princeton, N.J.: Princeton University Press, 1973), pp. 88–112.

9. Farrell E. Bloch and Mark S. Kuskin, "Wage Determination in the Union and Nonunion Sectors," *Industrial and Labor Relations Review*, January 1978, pp. 183–92.

10. Sandra L. Mason, "Comparing Union and Nonunion Wages in Manufacturing," *Monthly Labor Review,* May 1971, pp. 25–26.

11. See Press Release 76-940, "The Bureau of Labor Statistics Introduces the First Measure of Wage and Salary Rate Trends from Its New Employment Cost Index" (Washington, D.C., June 18, 1976).

12. U.S. Department of Labor, Bureau of Labor Statistics, Bulletin 2002, *Productivity Indexes for Selected Industries* (Washington, D.C.: GPO, 1978), table 12, p. 21.

13. Gladys L. Palmer, *Union Tactics and Economic Change* (Philadelphia: University of Pennsylvania Press, 1932).

14. George P. Shultz and Charles A. Myers, "Union Wage Decisions and Employment," *American Economic Review*, June 1950, pp. 362–80.

15. Peter Henle, "Reverse Collective Bargaining? A Look at Some Union Concession Situations," *Industrial and Labor Relations Review*, April 1973, pp. 956–68.

16. U.S. Department of Labor, Bureau of Labor Statistics, Report 546, *Collective Bargaining in the Airline Industry* (Washington, D.C., 1979), p. 3.

17. Between July 1971 and July 1977, union wage scales in the building trades advanced at an average annual rate of 6.7 percent; the corresponding figure for adjusted average hourly earnings in the private nonfarm economy was 8.6 percent.

18. A good exposition of monopsony will be found in Allan M. Cartter, *Theory of Wages and Employment* (Homewood, Ill.: Richard D. Irwin, 1959), pp. 60–74.

19. An attempt to compute employer concentration ratios for unskilled and semiskilled labor in 1,774 labor market areas for the late 1940s concluded that in a great many areas the ratio was quite low. Apparently firms discount or neglect monopsonistic gain as a location factor. See Robert L. Bunting, *Employer Concentration in Local Labor Markets* (Chapel Hill, N.C.: University of North Carolina Press, 1962).

20. See George Meany, "What Labor Means by 'More,' " *Fortune,* March 1955, pp. 92–93, 172, 174, 176.

Chapter 10

1. U.S. Department of Labor, Women's Bureau, Bulletin 267, *State Minimum Wage Laws and Orders,* part 1. *Historical Development and Statutory Provisions* (Washington, D.C.: GPO, 1958). See also Harry A Millis and Royal E. Montgomery, *Labor's Progress and Some Basic Labor Problems* (New York: McGraw-Hill, 1938), pp. 278–356.

2. See Elizabeth Brandeis, "Organized Labor and Protective Labor Legislation," in Milton Derber and Edwin Young (editors), *Labor and the New Deal* (Madison, Wis.: University of Wisconsin Press, 1957), pp. 217–30.

3. Dorothea Tuney, "Ten Years Operations under the Fair Labor Standards Act," *Monthly Labor Review*, September 1945, pp. 271–74.

4. Jack I. Karlin, "Economic Effects of the 1966 Changes in the FLSA," *Monthly Labor Review*, June 1967, pp. 21–25.

5. Peyton Elder, "The 1977 Amendments to the Federal Minimum Wage Law," *Monthly Labor Review*, January 1978, pp. 9–11.

6. U.S. Department of Labor, Bureau of Labor Statistics, Bulletin 2009, *Industry Wage Survey: Contract Cleaning Services, July 1977* (Washington, D.C.: GPO, 1978), table 3, pp. 9–10.

7. U.S. Department of Labor, Bureau of Labor Statistics, Bulletin 1987, *Industry Wage Survey: Hosiery, July 1976* (Washington, D.C.: GPO, 1977), table 3, p. 7, and table 21, p. 28.

8. Clarence Heer, *Income and Wages in the South* (Chapel Hill, N.C.: University of North Carolina Press, 1930), p. 35.

9. H. M. Douty, "Regional Wage Differentials: Forces and Counterforces," *Monthly Labor Review*, March 1968, pp. 74–81.

10. George J. Stigler, "The Economics of Minimum Wage Legislation," *American Economic Review*, June 1946, pp. 358–65. See also the communication on this and a related article by Richard A. Lester, and rejoinders by Fritz Machlup and George J. Stigler, *American Economic Review*, March 1947, pp. 135–57.

11. See communications on "Employment Effects of Minimum Wages" from Richard A. Lester and John M. Peterson, *Industrial and Labor Relations Review*, January 1960, pp. 254–73. At issue were two articles by Peterson: "Employment Effects of Minimum Wages, 1938–50," *Journal of Political Economy*, October 1957, pp. 412–30; and "Employment Effects of State Minimum Wages for Women: Three Historical Cases Reexamined," *Industrial and Labor Relations Review*, April 1959, pp. 406–22.

12. Sar A. Levitan and Richard S. Belous, *More Than Subsistence: Minimum Wages for the Working Poor* (Baltimore: Johns Hopkins University Press, 1979). I am indebted to Professor Levitan for an opportunity to read the manuscript of this study prior to publication. See also, by the same authors, an article entitled "The Minimum Wage Today: How Well Does It Work?" *Monthly Labor Review*, June 1979, pp. 17–21.

13. The account here is based largely on H. M. Douty, "Some Effects of the $1.00 Minimum Wage in the United States," *Economica*, May 1960, pp. 137–47. A complete list of the relevant Bureau of Labor Statistics studies is given in note 1 in that article.

14. Norman J. Samuels, "Plant Adjustments to the $1 Minimum Wage," *Monthly Labor Review*, October 1958, pp. 1137–42.

15. See, for example, R. H. Tawney, *The Establishment of Minimum Rates in the Tailoring Industry under the Trade Boards Act of 1909* (London: G. Bell and Sons, 1915), p. 254.

16. For an analysis of problems in econometric research on the employment effects of minimum wages, see Robert S. Goldfarb, "The Policy Content of Quantitative Minimum Wage Research," *Proceedings*, 27th Annual Winter Meeting, Industrial Relations Research Association, 1974, pp. 262–68; and Levitan and Belous, op. cit., chap. 4.

17. Perhaps the most extreme statement of the case for the minimum wage as the major cause of the increase in teenage unemployment will be found in Yale Brozen, "The Effect of Statutory Minimum Wage Increases on Teen-Age Employment," *Journal of Law and Economics*, April 1969, pp. 109–22.

18. Hyman B. Kaitz, "Experience of the Past: The National Minimum," in U.S. Department of Labor, Bureau of Labor Statistics, Bulletin 1657, *Youth Unemployment and Minimum Wages* (Washington, D.C.: GPO, 1970), p. 45.

19. Marvin Kosters and Finis Welch, "The Effects of Minimum Wages on the Distribution of Changes in Aggregate Employment," *American Economic Review*, June 1972, p. 330.

20. Jacob Mincer, "Unemployment Effects of Minimum Wages," *Journal of Political Economy*, August 1976, part 2, pp. S87–S104.

21. Edward M. Gramlich, "Impact of Minimum Wages on Other Wages, Employment, and Family Incomes," *Brookings Papers on Economic Activity*, 2, 1976, pp. 409–51.

22. Ibid., p. 450.

Chapter 11

1. The filtration of Keynesian ideas through economists to government policy officials in the United States is interestingly traced by Robert Lekachman in *The Age of Keynes* (New York: Random House, 1966).

2. See Henry Phelps Brown, *The Inequality of Pay* (Berkeley and Los Angeles: University of California Press, 1977), chap. 10, for a summary statement of the sources of pay inequality and the possibilities of its reduction. The volume as a whole provides a careful analysis of this important question.

Index